Ed Speak

A Glossary of Education Terms, Phrases, Buzzwords, and Jargon

Also by Diane Ravitch

The Great School Wars: A History of the New York City Public Schools

The Revisionists Revised: A Critique of the Radical Attack on the Schools

The Troubled Crusade: American Education, 1945–1980

The Schools We Deserve: Reflections on the Educational Crises of Our Times

What Do Our 17-Year-Olds Know? A Report on the First National Assessment of History and Literature (coauthor)

The American Reader (editor)

The Democracy Reader (coeditor)

National Standards in American Education: A Citizen's Guide

Left Back: A Century of Battles Over School Reform

The Language Police: How Pressure Groups Restrict What Students Learn

The English Reader: What Every Literate Person Needs to Know (coeditor)

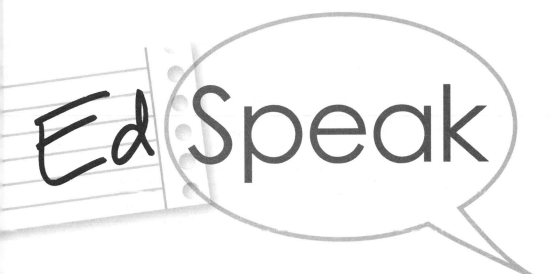

Ed Speak

A Glossary of Education Terms, Phrases, Buzzwords, and Jargon

DIANE RAVITCH

Association for Supervision and Curriculum Development
Alexandria, Virginia USA

Association for Supervision and Curriculum Development
1703 N. Beauregard St. • Alexandria, VA 22311-1714 USA
Phone: 800-933-2723 or 703-578-9600 • Fax: 703-575-5400
Web site: www.ascd.org • E-mail: member@ascd.org
Author guidelines: www.ascd.org/write

Gene R. Carter, *Executive Director;* Nancy Modrak, *Director of Publishing;* Julie Houtz, *Director of Book Editing & Production;* Miriam Goldstein, *Project Manager;* Reece Quiñones, *Senior Graphic Designer;* Valerie Younkin, *Desktop Publisher;* Dina Murray Seamon, *Production Specialist/Team Lead*

All Web links in this book are correct as of the publication date below but may have become inactive or otherwise modified since that time. If you notice a deactivated or changed link, please e-mail books@ascd.org with the words "Link Update" in the subject line. In your message, please specify the Web link, the book title, and the page number on which the link appears.

ASCD Member Book, No. FY07-9 (August 2007, P). ASCD Member Books mail to Premium (P), Comprehensive (C), and Regular (R) members on this schedule: Jan., PC; Feb., P; Apr., PCR; May, P; July, PC; Aug., P; Sept., PCR; Nov., PC; Dec., P.

PAPERBACK ISBN-13: 978-1-4166-0575-1   ASCD product #107072

Also available as an e-book through ebrary, netLibrary, and many online booksellers (see Books in Print for the ISBNs).

Quantity discounts for the paperback edition only: 10–49 copies, 10%; 50+ copies, 15%; for 1,000 or more copies, call 800-933-2723, ext. 5634, or 703-575-5634. For desk copies: member@ascd.org.

Library of Congress Cataloging-in-Publication Data
Ravitch, Diane.
    Edspeak : a glossary of education terms, phrases, buzzwords, and jargon / Diane Ravitch.
        p. cm.
    ISBN 978-1-4166-0576-8 (hardcover : alk. paper) — ISBN 978-1-4166-0575-1 (pbk. : alk. paper) 1. Education—United States—Dictionaries. 2. Education—United States—Acronyms—Dictionaries. I. Title.
    LB15.R285 2007
    370.3—dc22
                                                                        2007011242

16 15 14 13 12 11 10 09 08 07   1 2 3 4 5 6 7 8 9 10 11 12

For Mary

EdSpeak:
A Glossary of
Education Terms, Phrases,
Buzzwords, and Jargon

Preface

Every profession has its own language. Law, medicine, science, business, economics, psychology, sociology—each of these fields has evolved a specialized vocabulary that its members use to communicate with one another. Perhaps this language is necessary to discuss sophisticated ideas that are beyond the understanding of the average citizen; perhaps not. The result, if not the intent, is to mystify the public.

Education is no exception. Like those of other professions, the language of education is often incomprehensible to those outside the field. But more than other professions, education should strive to be intelligible to nonprofessionals. Educators must be able to speak clearly and intelligibly to all those who care about what happens in classrooms. It matters not only for the well being of students but also for the well-being of public education. Parents and citizens who are likely to vote on bond issues or to serve on local school boards need to understand the language of education, just as newcomers to and even veterans in the profession do.

I first encountered the strange tongue of education many years ago, when I started my graduate studies at Teachers College, Columbia University. Everyone, it seemed, understood the meaning of these unfamiliar words except me. I thought I would never be able to master this vocabulary because new terms were constantly popping up. Because I had been a journalist before I went to graduate school, I had a yearning to demystify what I learned. When I wrote books and articles, I purposely avoided jargon and buzzwords and tried to write in plain English for the larger public.

EdSpeak is my attempt to explain in everyday language the esoteric terms, expressions, and buzzwords used in U.S. education today. Some of these terms are multisyllabic replacements for simple, easily understood words; others describe government programs or the arcane technology of testing. I also added biographies of a few key figures who shaped the philosophy and practice of education, with only one proviso: no biographies of living persons. I decided to prepare this glossary so that others—be they parents, aspiring professionals, administrators, teachers, or just regular readers—would not be puzzled when they heard an unfamiliar term from a member of the profession.

Clearly, I am not alone in my desire to explain what the jargon means: in recent years, the *New York Times*, the *Washington Post*, and the *Los Angeles Times* have all published articles about the exotic and mysterious language spoken by educators. There is even an online education jargon generator (www.sciencegeek. net/lingo.html) that invites visitors to "amaze your colleagues with finely crafted phrases of educational nonsense!" A recent visit to the Web site reaped the following expressions: "leverage school-to-work learning styles," "target open-ended life-long learning," and "enable developmentally appropriate units." A reader might actually encounter some of these phrases in a pedagogical journal without knowing what they mean. Sometimes, I am sorry to say, such expressions are simply long-winded ways of sounding impressive without saying anything at all.

All this pedagogese has a relatively long pedigree: educators first began to use specialized terms at the beginning of the 20th century. At that time, the new profession of education psychology was attempting to make a science of education practice and, accordingly, began creating specialized, scientific-sounding terms. For many years, psychologists wrote and spoke about "laws of learning," for example, which were supposed to be immutable but are now forgotten. In the 1920s, pedagogues created a new vocabulary to describe child-centered learning, individualized instruction, and romantic views of the child; many of these terms have survived to this day, still sounding newly minted after almost a century of usage. In fact, media reports abound about new schools that embody policies—such as no tests, no textbooks, or no predetermined curriculum—that were hailed as innovative more than 100 years ago! Still more terminology was added by psychologists of education, who thought that their tests would make schooling a rational enterprise, and by sociologists of education, who saw the schools as a means to shape children to assume their foreordained roles in society. More recently, school language has been broadened by litigation about desegregation, adequacy, and equity. Even more terms have been added to the education glossary because of federal legislation, testing, and new currents in pedagogy.

My principal concern while writing this glossary was that I would leave out important terms, although this is somewhat inevitable, seeing as new terms seem to emerge almost magically on a daily basis. Almost every day, I come across another word or term that probably should have been added but has not yet achieved wide usage. It is also very likely—indeed, certain—that some words or phrases in this glossary will become obsolete, such as those that refer to federal programs that may or may not be renewed. Thus, I invite readers to submit new terms, as well as any current ones that I may have missed. I hope to update this book periodically, and I have no doubt that future editions will reflect this evolving language.

In a work of this kind, there are inevitably debts to fellow scholars. I owe an enormous debt to Robert D. Shepherd, who shared his vast knowledge of education terminology with me. I also thank the following people, who have suggested words or given me definitions of specialized terms: Williamson Evers, Chester E. Finn Jr., Eric Hanushek, E. D. Hirsch Jr., Deborah Meier, and Herbert Walberg. In addition, I thank Rita Kramer and J. Wesley Null for having read the entire manuscript and offering helpful suggestions.

I first had the idea to write this glossary while participating in a meeting of the Koret Task Force at the Hoover Institution at Stanford University. The members of the task force encouraged me to move forward, as did John Raisian of Hoover. I am immensely grateful for the support of the Hoover Institution and the Earhart Foundation.

I thank the Association for Supervision and Curriculum Development for publishing the glossary. My thanks go to Mary Butz for connecting me to Mary Ellen Freeley of ASCD, who in turn introduced me to Agnes Crawford, who embraced the concept of this glossary. I owe special thanks to Nancy Modrak, director of publications at ASCD, who enthusiastically supported the book. I was very lucky to have Miriam Goldstein as editor; she has been a considerate, careful, and attentive editor of what is surely a nontraditional manuscript.

Diane Ravitch
Brooklyn, New York

abecedarian: A student who is first learning the alphabet, usually a young child. This term was commonly used in the 17th century to refer to the youngest learners. It has also been adopted by a preschool program for low-income children in Chapel Hill, North Carolina, called the Abecedarian Early Childhood Intervention Project.

ability: Competence in doing something, either mental or physical. Psychometricians (experts in the design and analysis of tests) often contrast ability, which denotes whatever an individual is *currently* able to do, with aptitude, which refers to what an individual is *potentially* able to do.

ability grouping: The practice of assigning students to classes on the basis of their past achievement or presumed ability to learn. In schools that use ability grouping, low-performing students will be in one class, high-performing students in another, and average-performing students in yet another. This grouping by ability is called *homogeneous grouping*, whereas the practice of mixing students of different abilities in the same class is called *heterogeneous grouping*. Some schools group students by ability in certain subjects, like mathematics, but not in others, like social studies or English. Researchers disagree about whether ability grouping is beneficial. Advocates say that a certain amount of grouping is not only inevitable but also better for students. Many teachers find it daunting to teach classes with a wide range of ability because they must worry about boring students at the high end of ability while moving too rapidly for students at the other extreme. Critics of ability grouping contend that those placed in lower tracks encounter low expectations and are not sufficiently challenged. They also say that in most subject areas, students with lower or higher skills have much to learn from one another. See also **homogeneous grouping; tracking**. Contrast **detracking; heterogeneous grouping**.

abstinence education: An educational program premised on the view that family life and sex education courses should teach students that sexual intercourse is inappropriate for young, unmarried people. Advocates say that adults must communicate an unambiguous message that sex outside marriage is dangerous because of the risks of unwanted pregnancy and sexually transmitted diseases, such as AIDS. Critics of abstinence-only programs say the programs ignore the reality of widespread sexual activity among teenagers and deprive teens of information they need to protect themselves physically and emotionally.

academic achievement: The relative success of students in learning and mastering the school subjects that they study, as measured by tests of the knowledge and skills that were taught. Some educators believe that academic achievement should include a broader sample of performances than just test scores.

academic freedom: The freedom of educators to teach and to conduct research without fear of political reprisal, as well as the freedom of students to learn without fear of indoctrination or intimidation. Academic freedom for scholars involves both rights and responsibilities. Professors who assert their rights and freedoms have a responsibility to base their conclusions on competent scholarship and to present them in a dignified manner. Although they may express their own opinions, they are duty-bound to set forth the contrasting opinions of other scholars and to introduce their students to the best published sources on the topics at issue. In other words, professors may express their own views, but they must do so in a spirit of impartial scholarly inquiry, without imposing them on their students. Correlatively, students have the right to study under the guidance of qualified and unbiased faculty and to express their views without fear of any form of retribution.

academic press: The quality of the school environment—incorporating policies, practices, norms, and rewards—that produces high student achievement. A school with the right amount of academic press will have high but reasonable expectations for students, encouraging them to study and apply themselves to their schoolwork. Too much academic press and students will complain about the pressure; too little, and students will ignore their studies.

accelerated classes: Advanced classes in which highly motivated students study subjects and topics that are beyond their grade level. The term is also used to refer to intensive remedial classes intended to bring over-age, low-performing students up to their grade level. It is symptomatic of the education field's tendency toward euphemism that the same term is used to describe classes for students at both extremes of ability.

accelerated schools: A school reform in which all students in a school are given the enriched and challenging instruction ordinarily given only to gifted and talented students. Henry Levin of Stanford University (subsequently of Teachers College, Columbia University) designed a program called the Accelerated Schools Project to incorporate this approach; it was adopted in hundreds of schools across the United States. Its purpose was to improve education in urban schools serving many students designated as at risk of failure. Levin held that these schools' customary focus on remediation and basic skills depressed achievement and that students would make greater progress if exposed to the methods and topics usually reserved for gifted students.

accessing skills: The skills to seek and find information on the Internet, often taught in school.

accommodations: Changes in the design or administration of tests in response to the special needs of students with disabilities or students who are learning English. The term generally refers to changes that do not substantially alter what the test measures. The goal is to give all students equal opportunity to demonstrate their knowledge. Typical accommodations include allowing a student to take more time on a test, to take a test with no time limits, to receive large-print test booklets, to have part or all of a test read aloud, to use a computer to answer test questions, to have access to a scribe to write down the student's answers, to use Braille forms of the assessment, or to have access during the test to an English language dictionary.

accountability: The concept that individuals (e.g., students, teachers, or administrators) or organizations (e.g., schools, school districts, or state departments of education) should be held responsible for improving student achievement and should be either rewarded for their success or sanctioned for their lack of success in doing so. In education, accountability requires measurable proof that teachers, schools, districts, and states are teaching students efficiently and well. Usually this proof takes the form of student success rates on various tests. In recent years, most accountability programs have been based on state curriculum standards and state tests derived from those standards. Other accountability measures include student dropout rates, graduation rates, college entrance rates, samples of student work, and longitudinal studies of former students. Some critics of current accountability schemes advocate testing samples of schools rather than testing all students.

accountable talk: Talk by students about what they are learning, supported by evidence from the discipline of study (for example, documentary sources in history or proofs in mathematics). This pedagogical approach, designed by University of Pittsburgh researcher Lauren Resnick, is intended to encourage students to take responsibility for their own learning by discussing lessons with their peers and demonstrating that they can use knowledge appropriately.

accreditation: Official recognition that an individual or institution meets required standards. Accreditation of teachers is usually referred to as *licensing* or *certification*. Schools are accredited in two ways: by voluntary regional accrediting associations (such as the North Central Association Commission on Accreditation and School Improvement) and by state governments, which are legally responsible for public education. Most high schools seek and receive accreditation from their regional associations so that their graduates will be accepted by institutions of higher education. In recent years, some states have begun to withdraw state accreditation from schools with unacceptably low scores on state tests. Accreditation also refers to the process of certifying that institutions of higher education meet certain standards in relation to such matters as the qualifications of their faculty, the condition of their facilities, and the appropriateness of their curriculum. Most schools of education are accredited by either the National Council for Accreditation of Teacher Education or the Teacher Education Accreditation Council.

achievement: Accomplishment; the mastery of a skill or of knowledge as a consequence of the individual's effort, training, and practice.

achievement/ability comparison (AAC): The relationship between an individual's score on an achievement test and the scores of other students of similar ability (as measured by an ability test) on that same achievement test. If a given student's achievement test score is higher than those of students of similar ability, the AAC is said to be high; if the achievement score is about the same as the scores of similar-ability students, the AAC is middle; and if the student's score is lower, his or her AAC is low. The term assumes that one can accurately distinguish between *achievement* and *ability*.

achievement gap: Persistent differences in achievement among different groups of students as indicated by scores on standardized tests, grades, levels of educational attainment, graduation rates, and other data; also known as the *test-score gap*. Achievement on each of these measures strongly correlates with the socioeconomic status of a student's parents, especially their income and education. Race and ethnicity are also correlated with socioeconomic status. The achievement gap most frequently referred to in the United States is that between whites and Asian Americans on the one hand, and African Americans and Hispanics on the other. Needless to say, not all whites and

Asian Americans are high academic performers, and not all African Americans and Hispanics are low academic performers. Many researchers believe that a significant part of the gap may be attributed to poverty, high mobility rates, and low expectations. Narrowing or closing this gap is one of the rationales for standards-based reform, which aims to ensure that additional attention is paid to low-performing students and that expectations are similar for all students.

achievement levels: Performance levels that describe how well students did on a given test. The achievement levels on the federally sponsored National Assessment of Educational Progress are "basic" (partial mastery); "proficient" (solid academic performance); and "advanced" (superior performance). Students who perform poorly are rated as "below basic." These achievement levels and variations of them have been adopted by many states to describe levels of student performance on state exams. Achievement levels are established by panels of educators and other informed citizens who make a judgment about what students should know and be able to do at different grade levels. See also **advanced; basic; proficient**.

achievement tests: Assessments designed to measure knowledge and skills. An achievement test may assess general knowledge and skills or those related to particular school subjects. Norm-referenced multiple-choice tests, such as the Iowa Tests of Basic Skills, are intended to measure students' achievement in basic academic subjects. School officials use the test results to compare the scores of individual students and schools with those of others in the region, across the state, and throughout the United States.

acquisition-learning hypothesis: A theory that there are two ways to describe the learning of language. One way is subconscious acquisition, which is how infants learn their native language. The other is learning through instruction and study, which is the typical approach found in schools. Many teachers of foreign language now prefer the subconscious acquisition approach, which attempts to approximate living in a foreign country and being immersed in the use of the new language. See also **immersion**.

ACT: A set of college admissions tests and the organization that makes them, located in Iowa City, Iowa. The ACT is one of the two commonly used tests (the other is the SAT) designed to assess high school students' general educational development and their ability to complete college-level work. Although ACT originally stood for American College Testing, the organization shortened its official name to ACT in 1996 to reflect its broader scope. The ACT covers four skill areas: English, mathematics, reading, and science reasoning. Most colleges now accept either the SAT or the ACT for admissions purposes. More than 1 million college-bound high school students take the ACT each year. See also **SAT**.

action reflection process: A structured discussion held during regular teacher meetings in which participants focus on a limited topic. Leaders of the discussion may begin with a provocative statement or video, which is called an *action reflection tool*. The action reflection process was created by the Education Development Center of Newton, Massachusetts.

action research: The systematic investigation by teachers of some aspect of their work to help them improve their effectiveness. Action research requires that the participants identify a question or problem and then collect and analyze relevant data. It differs from conventional research in that the participants study an aspect of their own work in the classroom and intend to use the results themselves. For example, a teacher might decide to give students different assignments according to their assessed learning styles. If the teacher maintained records comparing student work before and after the change, he or she would be doing action research. If several educators worked together on such a project, this would be considered *collaborative action research*. Because of the personal interest of those who carry out action research, the results do not necessarily have credibility and are seldom generalized to other classrooms and schools.

active learning: Any situation in which students learn by doing rather than by sitting at their desks reading, filling out worksheets, or listening to a teacher. Active learning is based on the premise that if students are active, they will be highly motivated and will thus learn more. Some educators believe that the term refers to activities outside school, such as voluntary community service, or such in-school activities as role playing or conducting a mock trial. Others say that acting out a Shakespeare play in the classroom is active learning, and still others insist that reading a book or solving a mathematics problem is also active learning that requires the student's close attention.

active reading: A set of pedagogical strategies intended to get students involved in thinking about what they are reading. Active reading may involve any of a wide range of activities, such as underlining, outlining, predicting, summarizing, paraphrasing, connecting the reading to one's own experiences, visualizing, or asking questions about the content of the reading material.

additive bilingualism: A description of a bilingual program in which students gain proficiency in a new language while continuing to develop proficiency in their first language. The expectation is that students are not losing their first language but adding a second language. Contrast **subtractive bilingualism**.

adequacy: An approach to school funding that begins with the premise that the amount of funding schools receive should be based on some estimate of the cost of achieving the state's educational goals. This approach attempts to answer two questions: how much money would be enough to achieve those goals, and where would it be best spent? The concept of adequacy has been employed in litigation in a number of states where advocates of greater school funding argue that even if spending is equitable across districts, it is insufficient to ensure that all students reach the state's achievement standards. Determination of adequate levels of spending is frequently left to consultants who are hired by interested parties to estimate the "cost" of providing an adequate education. The ultimate decision about adequacy is rendered by courts and legislatures.

adequate yearly progress (AYP): An individual state's measure of yearly progress toward achieving state academic standards, as described in the No Child Left Behind (NCLB) legislation. Adequate yearly progress is the minimum level of improvement that states, school districts, and schools must achieve each year, as negotiated with the U.S. Department of Education. This progress is determined by a collection of performance measures that a state, its school districts, and subpopulations of students within its schools are supposed to meet if the state receives Title I, Part A, federal funding. The measures may include (1) specified percentages of students scoring "proficient" or "advanced" on state tests in English language arts and math; (2) participation of at least 95 percent of students in those tests; (3) specified Academic Performance Index scores or gains; and (4) for high schools, a specified graduation rate or improvement in the graduation rate. Student test scores must be disaggregated by gender, minority status, and eligibility for free or reduced-price lunch (a measure of poverty). According to NCLB, all public schools must reach universal proficiency in reading and math by the 2013–2014 school year. Critics doubt that a goal of 100 percent proficiency is feasible unless "proficiency" is redefined as something akin to functional literacy. See also **No Child Left Behind Act (NCLB)**.

ad hoc committee: A committee that is formed to complete a specific task, file a report, and then disband. The Latin phrase *ad hoc* means "for this" and, as commonly used, means "for a specific purpose."

Adler, Mortimer J. (1902–2001): A philosopher and author who dedicated himself to popularizing the great books and great ideas of Western civilization. A high school dropout, Adler took night classes at Columbia University, where he fell in love with philosophy. He failed to receive a bachelor's degree because he did not complete his physical education requirement, but he eventually earned a doctorate in philosophy, thus becoming possibly the first person to receive a doctorate without having first obtained either a high school diploma or a bachelor's degree. In 1930, he joined the faculty at the University of Chicago, where he teamed up with its president, Robert Maynard Hutchins, to promote the "Great Books" of the Western canon. In response, large numbers of people formed clubs to read and discuss the books designated by Hutchins and Adler as the touchstones of Western thought. Because of his devotion to perennial truths, Adler crossed swords with progressive educators in the 1930s. Over the course of his long life, he wrote dozens of books. For many years, he served as chair of the editorial board of *Encyclopædia Britannica*. In the early 1980s, hoping to promote serious reading and discussion in schools, Adler developed the Paideia Program, which emphasized coaching, seminars, and didactic instruction. See also **Great Books program; Hutchins, Robert Maynard (1899–1977); Paideia Program**.

adult education: Classes offered by school districts, community colleges, and other public and private organizations for people 18 years or older who are not enrolled in a traditional education institution. Such classes may or may not offer credit toward a degree. See also **continuing education**.

advanced: One of three achievement levels on the federally funded National Assessment of Educational Progress and on many state tests. *Advanced* represents superior academic performance. See also **achievement levels; basic; proficient**.

advanced placement (AP) courses: College-level courses offered by high schools to students who are above average in academic standing. Each course has a well-defined syllabus and an examination. Most colleges award college credit to students who pass one of the nationally standardized AP tests. Passing AP tests can save students time and tuition for entry-level college courses. The College Board, which administers the AP program, offers AP courses and examinations in many subject areas, including biology, calculus, and U.S. history. Examinations are graded on a five-point scale, 5 being the highest possible score. Students earn college credit by achieving a satisfactory score on an AP exam, usually a 3 or better. Many college admission officials favor students who have completed AP coursework and have passed the exams.

adverse reflection: A term found in California's "social content guidelines" to describe language that is critical of an individual or a group or that tends to ridicule, demean, or caricature an individual or a group. California will not endorse textbooks or other materials for use in its schools if they contain language that any group considers to contain adverse reflection. Sometimes historical fact creates an adverse reflection when it truthfully shows past behavior or cultural beliefs of groups that are contrary to contemporary standards. See also **social content guidelines**.

advisory: Organized daily meetings of one adult and a small group of students in middle school or high school. The adult, usually a teacher, gets to know all the students and gives them advice and acts as their advocate in the school. The advisory is designed to help students make wise choices in their academic and social lives and is expected to improve communication between home and school. Held during the school day, the advisory has taken on the function that was once assigned to the homeroom. See also **homeroom**.

affective education: Schooling that helps students deal with their emotions and values. This term is used to distinguish such schooling from *cognitive education*, which refers to academic knowledge and studies. Some would argue that the two are actually intertwined and that affective education increases students' readiness to learn by addressing their emotional problems.

affective filter: An emotional block in the student's mind that some researchers claim prevents learning. According to these researchers, teachers should do whatever they can to lower students' anxiety levels, increase their comfort levels, and raise their self-esteem so as to lower the affective filter and improve students' motivation to learn. Other researchers believe that a certain level of academic pressure is necessary to motivate students to learn.

affective objective: An instructional objective related to students' emotions, feelings, or values, indicated by such words as *interest*, *appreciation*, *enthusiasm*, *motivation*, and *attitudes*. Contrast **cognitive objective**.

Afrocentric education: A program based on the belief that students who are of African ancestry should have an education that is centered on the study of Africa. Advocates of this approach believe that studying the history, culture, and achievements of Africans will raise the self-esteem of African American students. Critics contend that such a restricted education will undermine the ability of these students to live in a diverse society and will set a divisive precedent for students of other ancestry groups. See also **Eurocentrism**.

after-school programs: Activities that take place after the official end of the school day, typically sponsored by the school, the school district, or community organizations. After-school programs include athletics, dramatic groups, technology education, art and music, and academic assistance activities. Due to the large increase in the number of working mothers in recent years, many children have no supervision between the hours of 3:00 and 6:00 p.m. Accordingly, many school districts and reformers have sought to increase the availability of after-school programs to make sure that children are in safe and stimulating environments during that time. The federal No Child Left Behind Act allocated $1 billion in funding for after-school programs (called 21st Century Community Learning Centers).

A–G curriculum: A four-year sequence of high school courses in California designed to prepare all students for higher education or the modern workplace. The curriculum includes such core subjects as English, mathematics, history, laboratory science, and a foreign language.

aha moment: The point at which a student suddenly understands what the teacher has been trying to get across. Some teachers describe the moment as a lightbulb going off in students' heads when they get the point of what they are learning. Adults also have aha moments, when they experience a flash of intuition that enables them to make decisions about their lives. Scientists refer to this sudden insight as the *eureka moment.*

algorithm: A systematic, step-by-step procedure for solving problems, especially mathematical problems. So, for example, if a student used addition, subtraction, division, or multiplication to solve a mathematical problem, he or she would be applying an algorithm. Many advocates of new approaches to teaching mathematics believe that students should seek multiple answers to mathematical questions rather than "right" answers and that the process of figuring out a solution is more valuable to students than learning a standard procedure that produces a right answer. Proponents of these new approaches also contend that calculators can solve algorithm problems faster than students can on their own, so students should use calculators in the classroom instead of relying on paper and pencil or solving problems "in their head." Advocates of traditional methods of teaching mathematics defend the teaching of algorithms and object to the use of calculators in the elementary grades. They contend that algorithms will always be valuable, that they must become habitual to be effective, and that many—perhaps most—mathematical questions do have right and wrong answers. They maintain that it is impossible for students to become creative solvers of mathematical problems until they have mastered the algorithms of mathematics and made their application automatic. Mastery of traditional algorithms, they say, is the surest path to long-term mathematical competency.

alignment: The degree to which curriculum, instruction, textbooks and other instructional materials, assessments, teacher preparation and professional development, and systems of accountability all reflect and reinforce the educational program's objectives and standards. The goal of alignment is to ensure that all the parts of the education system are working in concert to support student learning. The curriculum defines what is to be taught; textbooks and instructional materials contain the major lessons described in the curriculum; teacher education prepares teachers who have mastered what students are supposed to learn; professional development helps teachers extend their knowledge of the curriculum and their skill in communicating lessons to students; and assessments gauge what students were taught.

alignment-based reform: The effort to coordinate standards, teacher education, curriculum, instruction, testing, and accountability. In an aligned education system, the curriculum describes what students are expected to know and be able to do; teacher education programs produce teachers who know how to teach what students are expected to learn; teachers base their daily lessons on the course curriculum; textbooks teach what students are expected to learn; tests are based on the curriculum; and accountability systems report whether students are meeting the standards. Critics of alignment-based reform claim that such efforts are likely to exclude topics that appeal to particular students at particular moments in time.

alphabet: The 26 letters that make up the English language, beginning with *A* and ending with *Z*; also known as *the ABCs*. These letters are the building blocks of written words. In the 1840s, Horace Mann, known as the father of American public education, opposed the alphabet method of teaching reading, which required students to memorize the letters and combine them into words. He described the letters of the alphabet as "skeleton-shaped, bloodless, ghostly apparitions" that terrified children. In the 1960s, however, the Harvard reading researcher Jeanne Chall concluded after exhaustive research that knowledge of letters and their sounds is an essential first step in learning to read. See also **phoneme; phonics; whole language**.

alternate-route teacher: A teacher who has successfully completed an alternate certification process that permits qualified individuals lacking pedagogical credentials to earn them while teaching in the public schools, usually in a mentoring program. Such a program allows people to enter teaching after they have worked in other careers or to enter teaching without obtaining a degree in education.

alternative assessments: Tests of achievement or aptitude that do not rely on paper-and-pencil, multiple-choice, true/false, or short-answer questions to determine what students are learning and where they need help. Examples of alternative assessments include developing a special report or project, creating a portfolio (a collection of work), or performing a demonstration that exhibits one's knowledge and skills, the equivalent of a road test for drivers.

alternative certification: A license to teach acquired through a nontraditional route. Customarily, prospective teachers are expected to earn specific education credits or degrees in education to gain state certification. Alternative certification developed in the 1980s and 1990s as a way for individuals to become teachers without having to complete an undergraduate or graduate program in teacher education. Alternative certification takes into account an individual's background and experience and usually requires the candidate to pass a test and to receive some professional training in the first years of teaching. Alternative certification is most common in urban school systems that have difficulty hiring enough regularly qualified teachers. For example, Teach for America recruits recent college graduates to teach for two years in urban schools. Advocates claim that such programs provide a way for bright, idealistic young people to make a needed and worthy contribution. Critics contend that teaching requires extensive preparation to gain knowledge of child development and pedagogy and that such shortcuts undermine efforts to make teaching a true profession. See also **certified employees; teacher certification**.

---

alternative instruction room: A room where school officials send students who have misbehaved in school, usually for a few hours or days. See also **detention; reflection room**.

---

alternatively abled: A term denoting people with various handicapping conditions, coined to avoid use of words like *disabled* and *handicapped*. This euphemism is used in the social content guidelines of the state of California. See also **social content guidelines**.

---

alternative schools: Schools that serve students who have been unsuccessful in regular public schools or who have been expelled from regular public schools because of their misbehavior. Alternative schools are usually high schools; they are generally smaller and more personalized than regular public schools and are supposed to offer individualized programs and social services. They may operate under different governing principles than conventional schools and may be run by nonprofit or for-profit organizations other than local school boards.

American Diploma Project: A program intended to prepare high school graduates for college and work. Many states have joined the project and agreed to align their standards, curricula, assessments, and graduation requirements with the expectations of higher education and employers. The project was established by Achieve, the Thomas B. Fordham Foundation, and the Education Trust.

American Federation of Teachers (AFT): One of the two major national teacher unions (the other is the National Education Association). Founded in 1916, the AFT represents about 1.3 million teachers, school support staff, higher education faculty and staff, health care employees, and state and municipal employees. The AFT is affiliated with the AFL-CIO.

America's Choice: A school reform program created by Marc Tucker and the National Center on Education and the Economy, based on study of schooling in other nations. This whole-school redesign is based on the idea that instruction, assessment, teacher training, and professional development should be aligned with curricular standards. Several hundred schools in the United States have adopted this reform model.

a mile wide and an inch deep: A characterization of the mathematics curriculum in the United States, usually attributed to William Schmidt of Michigan State University. The phrase is often applied to any curriculum or course of study that covers so much material that it is too broad and too superficial for students to comprehend and remember what they have studied. See also **coverage**.

analysis chart: A graphic displaying the parts of something that may or may not show relations among those parts and between individual parts and the whole. For example, a student might make an analysis chart prior to writing a character sketch by creating rows or columns labeled Background, Relations with Others, Personality, Appearance, Education, and Social Class and then filling in each part. A particular type of analysis chart often used in writing classes is the *sensory details chart*, which contains rows or columns labeled Sight, Sound, Taste, Smell, and Touch. A student might create such a chart to gather details before writing a descriptive piece about an interesting locale that he or she has visited—for example, the Brooklyn Bridge or Venice Beach.

anecdotal notes: A teacher's description of student behavior and progress based on classroom observation, or a supervisor's description of teacher performance in the classroom.

annual measurable objective (AMO): A measurement used to determine compliance with the federal No Child Left Behind Act. The law requires states to develop annual measurable objectives that will determine whether a school, a district, or the state as a whole is making adequate yearly progress toward the goal of having all students proficient in English language arts and mathematics by 2014. Critics believe that this goal is impossible to meet.

application: The practical use of school-learned knowledge and skills in the "real world."

apportionments: Funds that federal or state governments distribute to Local Education Agencies or other government units according to certain formulas.

aptitude: Characteristics, whether native or acquired, that indicate an individual's ability to learn or to develop proficiency in some particular area, if given appropriate education or training.

aptitude tests: Assessments that measure general academic (scholastic) ability, like the SAT; special abilities (e.g., verbal, numerical, mechanical, or musical); or "readiness" for learning. Aptitude tests may measure previous learning and be used to predict future performance, usually in a specific field, such as a foreign language, shorthand, or nursing. In general, tests of aptitude predict whether students are likely to learn certain things, as opposed to achievement tests, which measure what they have already learned. The differences between aptitude tests and achievement tests are not always clear-cut.

articulation: The attempt to create a seamless transition from one part of the education system to the next—for example, from middle school to high school or from high school to university—especially with regard to the curriculum.

assessment: A test. An assessment may be part of a system for testing and evaluating individual students, groups of students, schools, or districts. Different types of assessment instruments include achievement tests, minimum competency tests, developmental screening tests, aptitude tests, observation instruments, performance tasks, and authentic assessments. Assessments may contain questions in any of a number of formats. Common formats for standardized tests include multiple-choice, short response, and open-ended response. See also **test**.

assessment-driven: A description of curriculum content and teaching practices that are based on assessments used for accountability purposes. Educators who provide assessment-driven instruction start with the assessment and then figure out what students need to know and be able to do to be prepared for the assessment. Some would argue that ideally, the assessment should be based on curriculum standards developed by the district, the state, or even federal authorities, but when those standards are vague or nonexistent, teachers study the assessment itself, which has an implicit curriculum.

assistive technology (AT): Any technological device or product —hardware or software—that is used to increase, maintain, or improve the functional capabilities of individuals with disabilities.

at-risk students: Students who are in danger of failing in school and becoming academically disadvantaged in comparison with their peers. They may be labeled "at risk" on the basis of such information as test scores, attendance, and discipline records. Students at risk have a higher-than-average probability of dropping out of school. A disproportionate number of at-risk students are homeless or come from low-income, inner-city homes; are not fluent in English; or have special needs and emotional or behavioral difficulties. Substance abuse, juvenile crime, poverty, and lack of adult support all contribute to placing students at risk of failure. Most school districts have programs and specially designed schools (e.g., alternative schools, magnet schools, theme schools) to address the needs of these youngsters.

attention deficit disorder (ADD): A condition that interferes with a person's ability to concentrate and control impulses and behavior. Students diagnosed with ADD tend to have problems getting started on tasks (and staying on them) and focusing on conversations or activities; they may be disorganized, impulsive, easily distracted, fidgety, and restless. They may also find it difficult to use their short-term working memory and access recall and to manage their emotions appropriately. Attention deficit hyperactivity disorder (AD/HD) describes a condition that interferes with a person's ability to regulate activity level, inhibit behavior, and attend to tasks in developmentally appropriate ways. People with AD/HD may move rapidly from one task to another without completing any of them. Hyperactivity, a disorder of the central nervous system, also makes it difficult for affected students to control their motor functions. Many students with learning disabilities exhibit behaviors associated with attention problems but do not necessarily have ADD or AD/HD.

authentic assessments: Assessments that attempt to test students in a manner that replicates a real-life situation. So, for example, an authentic assessment in a business class might require students to prepare a business plan and present it to a group of peers pretending to be venture capitalists. Or a student might demonstrate understanding of a chemistry unit by testing local waters for pollution or oil spills. Test makers sometimes try to make their tests more authentic by including real-world problems, such as balancing a checkbook on a math test. Critics of authentic assessment contend that most such tasks are individualistic, cannot be compared, and are necessarily graded by subjective measures.

authentic engagement: Enthusiastic involvement of students in their schoolwork, as opposed to involvement motivated solely by fear of failure or by the desire to win extrinsic rewards, such as good grades.

authentic learning: Schooling related to real-life situations, as opposed to learning only from books, especially textbooks. Advocates of authentic learning emphasize the value of real-life problems and experiences, contending that what is taught in school has little relationship to anything people do in the world outside school or to the interests of students themselves; efforts to make learning more authentic are intended to overcome that problem. Authentic learning activities tend to involve the kinds of problems faced by adult citizens, consumers, or professionals and usually require teamwork, decision making, and problem solving. Critics are concerned that such an approach could discourage learning from books, which are an important part of education. An education that consisted only of authentic activities, the critics say, would leave students ignorant of history, literature, and philosophy, as well as of the principles of science and mathematics.

authentic literature: Trade books, newspapers, magazines, and student-written stories, as opposed to textbooks; literature that is presented in its entirety, without selection or bowdlerization. Some plays by Shakespeare included in high school anthologies are edited to remove sexual references, such as those found in *Romeo and Juliet*. The American Library Association and the National Council of Teachers of English have inveighed against censorship of texts, but without much success. Some people also use the term *authentic literature* to refer to writings by members of racial and ethnic minority groups. Such collections are presumed authentic in the sense that they represent the diversity of the population at large.

authentic task: A school assignment that is like a real-world problem, similar to one that might be encountered at home, while shopping, or in the workplace.

authorizing agency for charter schools: An organization empowered by state legislation to issue a charter to groups that wish to establish charter schools. Some states give this authority to the state board of education or to local boards of education, whereas others create a special board to authorize charter schools or permit universities to do so. The states in which there are multiple authorizing agencies tend to have larger numbers of charter schools.

autism: Pervasive developmental disability that involves the inability to interpret the emotions of others and that significantly affects verbal and nonverbal communication. Individuals with autism have difficulty with the social interaction necessary to ordinary functioning in social settings, including educational ones.

auxiliary services: Most of the services provided by schools that are nonacademic in nature, such as operations, food services, maintenance, transportation, security, and facilities.

average class size: The number of students in a given school or district divided by the number of classes. Because some teachers, such as reading specialists and special education teachers, have assignments outside the regular classroom, the average class size is usually larger than the pupil-teacher ratio. See also **pupil-teacher ratio.**

average daily attendance (ADA): The total number of days of student attendance divided by the total number of days in the regular school year. ADA is not the same as enrollment, or register, which is the number of students enrolled in each school and district. (This number is determined by counting students on a given day, usually in the fall.) ADA tends to be lower than enrollment due to such factors as students moving, dropping out, or staying home because of illness. Based on counts taken on predetermined dates during the school year, average daily attendance is a factor used by state and federal departments of education to determine how much money schools receive. See also **enrollment**.

aversive behavioral therapy: Extreme forms of discipline, such as electroconvulsive therapy, bodily restraints, food deprivation, noxious tastes, and white noise through earphones, sometimes used in boarding schools that treat children who are emotionally or psychologically troubled. The purpose is to have students associate an undesirable behavior with a strong feeling of dislike or disgust, thus reducing or eliminating that behavior. Such therapy is very controversial and is often banned or regulated by state authorities.

back to basics: A slogan used by those who believe that schools are neglecting the fundamental skills of reading, writing, and arithmetic. Sometimes, as in the case of the Council for Basic Education, proponents of back to basics are also advocates for liberal education, including science, history, and other school subjects that they believe have been ignored. However, some advocates of the basics would eliminate subjects that they consider unnecessary or controversial, like sex education, environmental education, and other allegedly nonessential studies.

backward mapping: A process in which educators determine what students need to know and be able to do at a selected end point, such as high school graduation, and then build the curriculum in earlier grades to reach those desired end goals. The purpose is to make sure that students are prepared when they reach the desired end point. Backward mapping is a concept often used by curriculum designers and staff developers. See also **Understanding by Design**.

Bagley, William Chandler (1874–1946): A prominent educational psychologist, philosopher, and teacher educator who spent most of his career at Teachers College, Columbia University. Bagley achieved renown in his profession for his advocacy of liberal education in the 1910s, when others preferred vocational education; for his criticism of IQ tests in the 1920s, when most educational psychologists embraced them; and for his criticism of child-centered progressivism, which disparaged curriculum planning. He was a leader of the Essentialist movement, which emphasized the importance of a well-educated teacher and a well-planned curriculum. See also **Essentialism**.

---

balanced literacy: An approach to reading instruction that emphasizes the primacy of constructing meaning from authentic texts while also including instruction in skills. Balanced literacy classes incorporate elements of whole-language instruction, such as the use of complete and authentic (as opposed to decodable or vocabulary-controlled) texts and the teaching of common sight words, as well as providing some instruction in phonics. Such classes employ diverse strategies, including read aloud sessions, word walls, guided reading, and reading circles. Advocates laud the method because it relies primarily on teacher judgment and initiative. Critics note that balanced literacy programs retain the spirit of whole-language instruction while including just enough phonics instruction to meet the requirements of state standards. See also **whole language**.

---

banking theory of education: A term implying that the teacher-led classroom, where teachers teach and students learn, is fundamentally oppressive. This concept, developed by Brazilian radical educator and theorist Paulo Freire in *Pedagogy of the Oppressed,* holds that the teacher's act of "filling" the students with predetermined knowledge is akin to banking; that it relies on the authority of the teacher and the passivity of the student; and that it undermines critical consciousness. See also **empty bucket approach**.

---

basal readers: Textbooks with a controlled vocabulary used to teach beginning reading. Basal readers contain fiction and nonfiction, written in language that is appropriate for specific grade levels.

---

baseline data: Information (such as student test scores) collected at the beginning of a program's implementation. These data can then be compared with the same students' test scores or other indicators at the conclusion of the program or after it has been in effect for a certain period of time to evaluate the effectiveness of the program.

basic: One of three achievement levels on the federally funded National Assessment of Educational Progress and on many state tests. *Basic* represents partial mastery of what students should know and be able to do. See also **achievement levels; advanced; below basic; proficient**.

basic education: (1) An education emphasizing basic skills, such as reading, writing, and arithmetic. (2) A solid liberal education, including history, literature, science, mathematics, the arts, and a foreign language.

Basic Interpersonal Communication Skills (BICS): The language used in everyday, face-to-face communication, in contrast to the language needed in a formal academic setting. It is sometimes called *playground language* or *everyday language*. Contrast **Cognitive Academic Language Proficiency (CALP)**.

basic skills: The fundamental skills of reading, writing, and arithmetic, which are needed to succeed in school and in everyday life. In mathematics, the basic skills are addition, subtraction, multiplication, and division; in English, the basic skills include reading, writing, listening, and speaking.

battery of tests: A group of tests. For example, the Iowa Tests of Basic Skills Complete Battery is a set of achievement tests on vocabulary, reading comprehension, language, mathematics, social studies, science, and sources of information. The individual tests in a battery are called *subtests*.

behavioral objective: An objective that describes the behaviors that students are supposed to learn in class, such as problem solving, explaining, and manipulating.

behaviorism: A psychological theory based on the idea that learning occurs when repetition of a stimulus triggers a response. Behaviorists believe that learning consists of habit formation.

Behaviorism supports the importance of incentives and sanctions, as well as drill and practice. Taken to its extreme, behaviorism can make school mechanical and rigid; however, a certain reliance on incentives (e.g., grades, awards, and diplomas) and sanctions (e.g., discipline policy) is necessary for the successful functioning of schools, like most other social institutions. Critics of behaviorist approaches contend that humans respond differently from laboratory rats and that the development of social behavior for a democratic society must rely more on internal discipline than on extrinsic rewards and punishments.

behavior modification: Actions or strategies devised to change the way a person customarily acts in certain situations. In the classroom, behavior modification may involve systematic use of rewards and punishments to shape students' classroom deportment. Such systems usually involve explicit objectives, careful record keeping, visible tracking of progress, and immediate feedback (i.e., rewards and penalties). Used largely in special education classes for behaviorally disturbed students, behavior modification is controversial. Critics claim that it makes students dependent rather than independent and that its principles rely too much on animal studies. Advocates contend that it is scientifically based and effective.

bell curve: The shape of an idealized normal (frequency) distribution that takes the form of a symmetrical bell in which the highest number of occurrences appear at the top of the bell (where the mode and the median converge) and the smallest numbers lie at the extremes. All norm-referenced tests are constructed so that the distribution of scores resembles a bell curve, but tests could be constructed to reflect other distributions of intelligence and achievement, not just a bell curve. *The Bell Curve* is also the title of a controversial book by Richard J. Herrnstein and Charles Murray that suggests that race is linked to IQ. See also **grading on the curve; normal curve.**

below basic: A description of a very low level of student performance on tests administered by the federal National Assessment of Educational Progress (NAEP). NAEP ranks student performance according to three achievement levels: advanced, proficient, and basic. *Basic* is defined as "partial mastery" of skills fundamental to proficient performance. *Below basic* is not actually an achievement level but a catchall label for student performance that does not attain even partial mastery of skills considered necessary for proficient performance. See also **achievement levels; advanced; basic; proficient**.

benchmark books: Books that are designed for specific reading levels, enabling students to select books that they are able to read and teachers to determine which books are appropriate for which students.

benchmark performances: Performance examples against which other performances may be judged.

benchmarks: Any specific, measurable goals or objectives for students to meet at various points during the school year. Benchmarks are sometimes represented by samples of student work, either from current students or from students from previous years. A set of benchmarks can be used as checkpoints to monitor student progress in meeting performance goals within and across grade levels.

Bestor, Arthur (1908–1994): A prize-winning historian who wrote scathing critiques of American education in the 1950s: *Educational Wastelands* and *The Restoration of Learning*. His books protested anti-intellectualism and the dumbing down of the schools. He was a founder of the Council for Basic Education, which advocated a liberal education for all students.

best practices: A phrase derived from the business sector to describe what are thought to be the most effective methods to improve productivity and profit. Assertions about best practices are not always grounded in impartial reviews of evidence about effectiveness. Advocates believe that best practices should be shared for the benefit of educators seeking solutions to specific problems. Critics regard the phrase as a term of art applied by partisans of different educational methods to advance their own favored approaches.

bias: A difference in test outcomes attributable to such demographic variables as gender, race, age, or socioeconomic status.

The charge of bias usually is a claim that test questions implicitly or explicitly favor one group over another group. A difference in outcomes could be due to a real difference in the tested population (one may have more education than another) or to a systematic error in the testing instrument. Test developers may decide that a test question is biased and eliminate it, even if the test question appears to be fair on its face, because students of one group persistently have less success in answering it than students of other groups.

bias and sensitivity review: Analysis of tests and textbooks by committees responsible for determining whether the materials contain content that might be explicitly or implicitly offensive, biased, or insensitive to any group of people. Such committees are created by test developers, textbook companies, and state and federal governments to screen educational materials and to eliminate potential sources of bias and insensitivity. Sensitivity reviewers analyze textbooks and stories to be used in standardized tests to make sure that they do not refer to controversial topics like evolution, abortion, or suicide and that they do not contain language that might offend feminists or members of racial, ethnic, or religious groups. These committees frequently edit, bowdlerize, or delete literary selections to remove ideas, images, or language that someone might find offensive.

bias guidelines: The rules used by bias and sensitivity reviewers as they screen educational materials for content that might prove offensive to any minority groups or political constituencies. Such guidelines are written by test publishers, state education agencies, and other education organizations. They contain long lists of words, images, and topics that cannot be used in textbooks or tests.

bicultural education: A program or activity intended to teach students to identify with the cultures of two different linguistic or ethnic or heritage groups. Being bicultural is not necessarily the same as being bilingual, and vice versa.

big books: Oversize books used to teach reading in the early grades. The idea of using big books was imported to the United States from New Zealand in the early 1970s. It is assumed that they are attractive to children because of their large type and colorful illustrations; many teachers use them for shared reading activities, when the teacher or a classroom aide reads with more than one child at the same time. Big books are often found in whole-language and balanced literacy classrooms.

bilingual education: School program that teaches English language learners all subjects in their native language while they are learning English. Advocates see bilingual education as a way to help students gain knowledge while becoming literate in two languages. Critics question such programs' value and effectiveness, contending that limited-English-proficient students' main priority should be to learn English—and learn *in* English. See also **dual immersion**.

bilingualism: The ability to speak and read two languages.

Bill and Melinda Gates Foundation: The largest philanthropic foundation in the history of the world, established by Microsoft founder Bill Gates to make strategic charitable contributions, mainly in the fields of public health and education. The Gates Foundation's decision to award more than $1 billion to districts that created small high schools or divided up large high schools spurred a nationwide movement for that goal in the early years of the 21st century.

Blaine amendment: A provision in three dozen state constitutions barring the allocation of public funds to religious schools. These state amendments were adopted after the defeat in 1875 of a similar amendment to the U.S. Constitution, proposed by James G. Blaine, Speaker of the House of Representatives. The state Blaine amendments were passed in the 1870s and 1880s during a period of intense anti-Catholic bigotry, when the public school was seen as a bulwark to preserve Protestant values.

Blob, the: A term originally derived from a 1958 science fiction movie of the same name in which an alien creature terrorized a small town. In education, the term was adapted in the mid-1980s by then–Secretary of Education William J. Bennett to refer derisively to the public education establishment. By the "education establishment," he and others meant the numerous organizations that represent teacher unions, administrators, and others who lobby in Washington, D.C., and state capitals for public education.

block grant: An allotment of money that is the sum of multiple special-purpose funds combined into one. A block grant tends to have fewer restrictions on how the money is spent than the original, disparate funding streams had, and it often combines funds that have similar purposes.

block scheduling: A way of organizing the school day, usually in secondary schools, into blocks of time longer than typical class periods. Instead of the traditional day that contains six, seven, or eight periods of 40–50 minutes each, students take fewer courses that last for approximately 90 minutes (or longer) each. Students end up taking the same number of classes, but they are not conducted for the entire school year. One block schedule model known as *4 × 4* consists of four 90-minute classes a day with course changes every 45 days (four times a school year). Others include the *alternate-day plan*, in which classes meet every other day for longer periods of time, and the *trimester plan*, in which students take two or three courses every 60 days. In some current school reforms, such as the Coalition of Essential Schools, one teacher will teach two related subjects in a 90- to 120-minute block for the full year, so that students have fewer teachers and teachers have fewer students. The advantage of block scheduling is that students and teachers have fewer classes to prepare for and experience fewer interruptions in the school day; advocates claim that longer blocks of time allow for more complex learning activities. Critics argue that much of the extra time is wasted, that the schedule may actually reduce overall course time, that students' attention spans waver over longer periods, and that the teaching of certain subjects suffers because of the absence of sequential courses taken over several years. Mathematics and foreign language, for example, are subjects that require sequential, cumulative development and continual reinforcement of prior learning; the ability to take such a course one semester and not the next leads to a discontinuity that may impair learning. See also **flexible scheduling**.

Bloom's taxonomy: A highly influential classification of education objectives developed in the 1950s by a group of researchers headed by Benjamin Bloom of the University of Chicago. Bloom's taxonomy identified three domains of skills: cognitive (mental skills, or *knowledge*); affective (growth in feelings or emotional areas, or *attitudes*); and psychomotor (manual or physical skills, or *skills*). Each of these domains is then subdivided into several categories ranging from the simplest to the most complex; for example, the categories in the cognitive domain go from *recall* to *comprehension* to *application* to *analysis* to *synthesis* to *evaluation*. Bloom's taxonomy has been widely used by teachers to improve their instruction; it helps them shape their lessons, understand the difficulty of what they are teaching, and ask clear questions in class.

Blue Ribbon School: A school that has won a designation of excellence from the U.S. Department of Education's Blue Ribbon Schools Program. The honor is based mainly on self-evaluation by participating schools.

bonus pay: Extra money for school district employees who perform extra duties or who are considered exemplary. Some districts and states pay teachers extra if they improve their students' academic performance (test scores); this is called *performance pay*. Teacher unions dislike performance pay because they consider it divisive and because some staff members (such as art teachers or school secretaries) will never qualify for a bonus based on test performance. See also **incentives for teachers; merit pay; performance incentive**.

bookend approach to education reform: A reform strategy that relies solely on standards and assessments as "bookends" for reform, without paying attention to what goes in between—curriculum and instruction, along with other factors that affect student academic achievement.

boot camp: A term borrowed from the military that refers to a physically and emotionally demanding institutional setting in which students must comply with clear instructions without excuses or delay.

bottom-up reform: School reform that begins at the level of the individual classroom and works its way up in the school system through example and persuasion, not compulsion or mandates. This approach is attractive in theory but seldom leads to systemwide change because of the multiplicity of inconsistent examples from what could be dozens or hundreds of bottom-up reforms in one district. Both bottom-up and top-down reforms have built-in limitations—the former because there is no assurance that they will be effective or replicable, the latter because they may wrongly impose mistaken programs on unwilling teachers. Contrast **top-down reform**.

brain-based education: An approach to schooling that claims to be grounded in research on the brain and human learning. Proponents of brain-based instruction seek to understand how the brain works and to apply these findings in the classroom. Neuroscientists, however, do not endorse brain-based applications in the classroom because brain research is still in its infancy and does not provide clear direction on how teachers should teach.

brain-compatible strategies: Instructional approaches that incorporate thinking processes and real-life activities in the classroom, make use of visual and auditory stimuli in addition to written materials, and engage higher-order thinking skills. Critics say that there is no scientific basis to such strategies and that they simply reflect the pedagogical preferences of advocates.

brainstorming: Thinking out loud with others about a problem or a challenge. The process generally entails discussing a wide range of ideas, writing them down, talking about them, analyzing them, and generating potential solutions. During brainstorming sessions, the teacher is supposed to withhold critical comments on the ideas proposed by students so as not to interfere with their thinking processes. This practice originated in the fields of business and science as a means of eliciting new ideas.

break-the-mold schools: A phrase associated with the New American Schools Development Corporation, a private group created by business leaders at the behest of the administration of President George H. W. Bush to stimulate the creation of innovative schools. Most of these new schools resembled existing schools, however, and they did not break many molds. See also **New American Schools Development Corporation (NASDC)**.

Brown v. Board of Education: A landmark 1954 ruling by the U.S. Supreme Court holding that racial segregation in public schools was unconstitutional. Under the guidance of the National Association for the Advancement of Colored People's Legal Defense Fund, students and parents in several different school districts challenged laws that required students of different races to attend different schools. The lead plaintiff in the case was Linda Brown, a student in Topeka, Kansas, who was not allowed to attend the public school in her neighborhood. The case combined legal challenges to racially segregated schools in Kansas, South Carolina, Delaware, Virginia, and the District of Columbia. The *Brown* decision overruled the *Plessy v. Ferguson* decision of 1896, which endorsed the principle of "separate but equal" as it applied to public transportation and, implicitly, to public schools and other public facilities and services. See also **Plessy v. Ferguson**.

Bullshit Bingo: A game that bored teachers play during professional development sessions. The attendee creates a grid on a piece of paper with five columns and five rows and then writes a different overused term or phrase in each block (e.g., *multiple perspectives, exemplars, data-driven,* and so on). Whenever a speaker uses one of these words or phrases, the attendee checks off the relevant box. When there are five blocks checked off horizontally, vertically, or diagonally, the game is "won." Also known as *Buzzword Bingo*.

bureaucracy: The departments and agencies that manage an organization's flow of information and funding, handle personnel issues, and transmit decisions from the top of a hierarchical structure to those below. Bureaucracies evolve as organizations, whether public or private, grow larger. Not many people would claim to like bureaucracy, but it is rare to find a large organization without such a system in place.

Bureau of Indian Affairs: A federal agency that provides education services to students of American Indian and Alaska Native ethnicity.

burnout: Teacher exhaustion and stress caused by the demands placed on them by unruly students, unsupportive administrators, inflexible mandates, unceasing paperwork, and other burdens that make teaching a difficult career. Teachers who "burn out" presumably leave the profession or retire.

---

busing: The practice of reassigning students from one part of a school district to another, or from one school district to another, for the purpose of changing the racial composition of both the receiving schools and the sending schools. In the late 1960s, the U.S. Supreme Court approved mandatory busing plans to reduce racial segregation wherever segregation had been imposed in the past by state or local authorities. Throughout the southern states and in some cities outside the South, students were transported by school bus from their neighborhoods to schools in different neighborhoods to change the racial composition of schools. Busing received overwhelming support from civil rights groups but was largely opposed by parents of white students who were reassigned involuntarily. In 1974's *Milliken v. Bradley* decision, the U.S. Supreme Court invalidated a desegregation plan that involved busing students between Detroit and the surrounding suburban districts, thus dramatically limiting the future of metropolitan busing plans. In the 1990s, federal courts began dissolving busing orders, either because the school district had complied with previous court requirements or because white flight from urban districts had eroded the ability of the city school systems to attain racial integration by continuing to reassign students. The term *busing* should not be confused with the customary voluntary transporting of students to the nearest local school, especially in suburban and rural communities.

---

buy-in: The willingness of teachers and administrators to accept the premises and goals of a new program and to implement it faithfully and wholeheartedly.

capacity building: The process of increasing the material or human resources of an institution (e.g., a school or school district) so that it can engage in continuous improvement.

capital outlay: Money spent for major physical improvements in a public school district, such as new buildings, renovations, reconstruction, or certain new equipment.

caps: (1) Limits on the number of charter schools that a state legislature will permit to open in the state. (2) Restrictions on the number of children eligible to participate in a public or private program, due to limited funds.

Cardinal Principles of Secondary Education: A report issued by the National Education Association's Commission on the Reorganization of Secondary Education in 1918, long considered to be the most influential curriculum document of the 20th century. It proposed to reorganize the high school curriculum around basic social functions of life instead of academic subjects. The main objectives of education, said the report, were health, command of fundamental processes, worthy home membership, vocation, citizenship, worthy use of leisure, and ethical character. Critics argued that the effect of the report was to support vocational education and undermine the academic curriculum. Defenders of the report said that it made universal high school education possible by providing alternatives to the academic curriculum for many students.

career education: Schooling that aims to prepare students for a job or vocation.

career ladder: In education, the progression by which an educator rises from the bottom rung of the ladder as a novice teacher to become a master teacher or an administrator.

career lattice: A term acknowledging that career moves by teachers and administrators may go up or down or sideways, not necessarily upward all the time.

Carnegie unit: A unit of academic credit in high school used in college admissions decisions. The measurement indicates how much academic course work a high school student has completed. One Carnegie unit is equal to a conventional 50-minute class attended five times per week throughout the school year. A one-semester course is worth one-half of a Carnegie unit. Students usually need at least 20 units to graduate from high school. Carnegie units were established and promoted in the early 20th century by the Carnegie Foundation for the Advancement of Teaching. The foundation won widespread adoption of Carnegie units by letting it be known that faculty in colleges that did not require the units for incoming students would not be eligible to participate in the foundation's new pension program. Some educators now oppose the use of Carnegie units, arguing that "seat time" is not necessarily a good measure of learning.

categorical programs: State or federal programs granting funds to qualifying schools or districts for specific children with special needs, such as the federal Title I program for low-income children. With limited exceptions, school districts are not supposed to mingle funds from categorical programs with general funds.

ceiling effect: The tendency of students at the top of the achievement scale not to increase their test scores dramatically because they have already reached "the ceiling," or the highest possible level of achievement. When scores in a high-performing school remain stagnant, it may be because there is relatively little room for improvement and virtually no room for large gains on the kinds of assessments being used.

celebrations of approximations: A term used by adherents of whole-language instruction meaning that the teacher should encourage students when their efforts are nearly, but not completely, correct.

central office: A school district's top-level management and its support staff, which may or may not be housed in a single office location; also called *district office*. The term *central office* typically refers to the superintendent, the school business administrator, assistant superintendents and business officials, districtwide directors, and their support staff.

certificate of completion: A document issued by a school district to a student stating that the student has completed the necessary courses for a high school diploma. Usually, such a certificate is issued to students who were unable to pass the district or state's graduation examination.

certified employees: Employees who are required by the state to hold some sort of official license or certificate; also called *credentialed employees*. Such employees include most administrators and full-time, part-time, substitute, and temporary teachers. Typically, states require teachers to have a bachelor's degree, to complete some additional coursework in pedagogy or in their academic subject, and to pass a qualifying test. See also **alternative certification; classified employees; teacher certification**.

chalk and talk: A derogatory term referring to the teaching style of educators who lecture to their classes and write on the blackboard. Those who use this negative description prefer a teaching style that is indirect and involves such practices as group work, one-on-one coaching, seminars, or collaborative learning, where the teacher is a facilitator and a coach, not one who directs student learning through a lecture-type approach. Critics of the direct approach believe, as a popular expression puts it, that the teacher should be "a guide on the side, not a sage on the stage." See also **guide on the side; sage on the stage**.

Chall, Jeanne (1921–1999): A major figure in the scientific study of reading. Chall wrote the definitive study of reading instruction, *Learning to Read: The Great Debate* (1967), in which she described the history of research about reading and concluded that most children need to learn to decode the language to read well. Her last book, published posthumously, was *The Academic Achievement Challenge*, which summarized her research of the previous 50 years; in it, she concluded that teacher-directed instruction was almost always more effective for student learning than child-centered instruction, especially for poor and disadvantaged students. For most of her career, Chall was a professor of psychology at the Harvard Graduate School of Education.

challenging vocabulary: Words that students don't know yet.

character education: Schooling that teaches children about basic human values, such as honesty, kindness, generosity, courage, freedom, equality, and respect. The goal of character education is to help students become morally responsible, self-disciplined citizens. Character education programs have been supported by federal, state, and local funding, as well as by foundations and civic organizations. Service learning is frequently part of a comprehensive character education program. See also **service learning**.

charter management organization (CMO): An organization that manages more than one charter school, sometimes in more than one state. Such organizations seek to create a professional business office that is able to meet the needs of multiple charter schools. Usually a CMO operates as a nonprofit entity. See also **educational management organization (EMO)**.

charter school: A publicly funded school that, in accordance with an enabling state statute, has been granted a charter exempting it from certain state or local rules and regulations. A charter school may be newly created, or it may previously have been a public or private school; it is typically governed by a group or an organization (e.g., a group of educators, a corporation, or a university) under a contract or charter with the state or local district. This governing organization may be nonprofit or for-profit. In return for public funding and autonomy, the charter school must meet accountability standards. A school's charter is reviewed periodically, typically every three to five years, and can be revoked if the school does not meet its goals or is poorly managed. A charter school is like a school district with only one school, managed by its own board of directors. Each state defines the requirements for charter schools somewhat differently in its enabling legislation.

cheating: Fraudulent actions committed by students to get better grades or test scores or by adults who seek to make their children, students, schools, or districts appear more successful than they really are. Students who cheat may commit plagiarism, surreptitiously bring the answers to test questions into an examination, or copy another student's answers during a test. On rare occasions, students have persuaded or paid others to take tests for them in situations where the test takers are anonymous. Adult cheating occurs when parents do their children's schoolwork, when teachers give students unearned grades, or when district officials inflate test scores or graduation rates. See also **plagiarism**.

chief state school officer: The highest-ranking official responsible for public schools in each state. Different states call their highest-ranking school administrator by different titles—state superintendent of education or commissioner of education, for example. The national organization of these officials is called the Council of Chief State School Officers.

child-centered education: A philosophy of education in which the students' interests—not the school's curriculum or the teacher's plan—set the instructional agenda. In a child-centered school, the activities of each classroom are determined by the interests, characteristics, and needs of the students, rather than by a set academic program that is common to all students in a school, district, or state. Child-centeredness is a defining feature of progressive education, especially the currently popular form known as constructivism. Progressive educators teach that the classroom is a setting for students' lives, rather than a place of study and instruction, and should therefore involve a high degree of pupil initiative. Child-centered classrooms avoid teacher domination, teacher lecturing, and teacher telling. In its most extreme form, the child-centered classroom is highly permissive, and students do what they want to do and decide what, when, and how to learn. Most child-centered classrooms, however, maintain a modicum of structure determined by the teacher while paying close attention to the interests and needs of the students. See also **learner-centered classroom; progressive education**. Contrast **teacher-centered instruction; teacher-directed classroom**.

child study movement: A movement in the late 19th and early 20th centuries that advocated the study of children's interests, emotions, needs, and physical development as the basis for determining their educational program. The child study movement was launched by psychologist G. Stanley Hall, who was the first president of the American Psychological Association and of Clark University in Worcester, Massachusetts. The movement enjoyed great popularity among teachers and parents in the early 20th century and brought increased attention to the needs of children. However, it eventually lost its luster because of the poor quality of the research on which it was based: much of the research consisted of interviews with children conducted by enthusiastic amateurs.

choice: A policy giving parents the right to decide where to send their children to school, rather than being required by law to send them to an assigned public school. Under the federal No Child Left Behind Act, school districts must permit students to transfer out of consistently low-performing or persistently dangerous schools, as defined by the state, but such choices are often limited due to the inadequate supply of available seats in good schools. Those who support school choice have advocated passage of laws allowing the development of charter schools, school vouchers, and other changes to promote parental choice of schools. Charter schools have proven to be less controversial than school vouchers as a form of school choice because voucher programs allow students to use public funding to attend religious schools; the mixture of public dollars and religious institutions invariably raises legal and constitutional issues and has restrained the growth of voucher programs. The small schools movement has led to increased opportunities for student choice, but critics worry that such choices will lead to increased racial/ethnic and class segregation, as some small schools give preference to students who are perceived as high-performing. See also **charter school; vouchers**.

chunking: The act of grouping what students are learning into manageable segments, making the material easier to learn than it would be as many discrete facts.

civic education: Education for good citizenship. This goal has always been important in U.S. public education, and schools have long been expected to teach students about their rights and responsibilities as citizens; how to participate in government; how local, state, and federal governments function; and how they as citizens can contribute to improve society. Responsibility for civic education has traditionally been assigned to civics and history classes, where students learn about the meaning of the Constitution and the Bill of Rights and the history of the United States' efforts to protect its freedoms and democratic way of life. In addition, there is a general expectation that every teacher and every class should teach children and adolescents how to work successfully in a social setting, how to resolve conflicts amicably, and how to behave respectfully toward other people.

Civil Rights Act of 1964: Federal legislation that prohibits discrimination on the basis of race or ethnicity by any program or activity that receives federal financial assistance. This legislation was passed to end legal discrimination, especially in the southern states, and banned segregation in schools, higher education, public transportation, public housing, and other public facilities. In the years following the act's passage, the U.S. Congress passed Title IX of the Education Amendments of 1972, Section 504 of the Rehabilitation Act of 1973, the Age Discrimination Act of 1975, and Title II of the Americans with Disabilities Act of 1990, which prohibited discrimination on the basis of gender, disability, or age.

classified employees: School employees who are not required to hold teaching credentials, including bus drivers, secretaries, custodians, instructional aides, and some management personnel. See also **certified employees**.

classroom-based assistance: The help provided to teachers by teacher trainers who are working in their classrooms.

classroom-based observations: Observations by teacher trainers of teachers at work in the classroom. The teacher trainers give the teachers feedback on their performance based on their observations.

classroom grouping: Action taken by school administrators to assign students to classes with others of similar ability (homogeneous grouping) or to classes with others whose abilities span a wide range (heterogeneous grouping). The term also refers to practices within the classroom that have similar intent. See also **ability grouping; detracking; heterogeneous grouping; homogeneous grouping; tracking**.

classroom management: The way a teacher organizes and administers routines to make classroom life as productive and satisfying as possible. Classroom management includes but is much broader than discipline. For example, teachers with good classroom management skills explain classroom routines and may even begin the school year by having students practice expected procedures as a way of minimizing disruptions and maximizing the time for instruction.

classroom trailers: Trailers located on school property and used as classrooms. Such trailers are a result of student enrollment outgrowing the classroom space available in the main school building. See also **portable classrooms**.

class size reduction: A policy to lower and limit the number of students in the classroom, usually adopted by a school district or a state. This policy is highly popular with parents and teachers. A longitudinal study in Tennessee called Project STAR showed that young children—especially African American children—make significant gains when they learn in small classes. Advocates of class size reduction say that it enables teachers to give more time and attention to each student and improve student achievement. Critics contend that because it requires more teachers and more classrooms, it is expensive and may cause a shortage of teachers and classrooms as well as lead to the hiring of teachers with emergency credentials.

closed-response item: A test question that has a single correct answer or a narrow range of acceptable answers. Most multiple-choice and true/false tests are closed-response. See also **multiple-choice item**. Contrast **constructed-response item; open-response item**.

cloze reading: A test or exercise of reading comprehension in which the student must supply words that have been purposely removed from a sample piece of writing.

cluster grouping: A way of organizing classes so that students remain with an assigned group for every class. Each cluster of students has a team of teachers, one from each of the following departments: English, mathematics, science, and social studies and, for some students, special education or bilingual education. Students are usually assigned to a cluster at random and stay with the same group throughout the school year.

coaching: A term borrowed from athletics to refer to any situation in which an experienced person helps a novice to learn a skill. The philosopher Mortimer Adler, who devised the Paideia Program, maintained that coaching is one of three basic modes of teaching (along with seminars and didactic instruction). The term is also widely used to describe expert educators (usually experienced teachers or principals) helping other teachers and principals to improve their practice.

Coalition of Essential Schools: A high school–university partnership founded by Theodore Sizer at Brown University in 1984. According to the coalition, schools must be tailored in unique ways to serve their particular communities as effectively as possible. Coalition schools adhere to a set of 10 governing principles that include helping young people learn to use their minds well; helping students focus on the mastery of a limited number of essential skills, intellectual habits, and areas of knowledge, rather than a shallow coverage of content knowledge; holding all students accountable for the same goals; using various teaching styles to accommodate the different ways in which students learn; maintaining a teacher-to-student ratio that permits teachers to know students as individuals; and arranging for competitive teacher salaries, as well as substantial planning and training time for teachers. To graduate, students are expected to demonstrate their mastery of certain skills and knowledge in ways decided on by the faculty and administrators, along with the community.

cocurricular activities: Studies or activities for students that take place outside the classroom but are supposed to bolster learning. Examples of cocurricular activities include outside lectures, seminars, workshops, debates, and community service programs.

code-switching: A term used to describe any switch among different languages, dialects, or registers during a conversation. Code-switching often occurs when bilingual people are talking to others who are bilingual in the same languages. It also occurs when people switch from a dialect of English to standard English or from informal conversational language to formal language.

Cognitive Academic Language Proficiency (CALP): Student proficiency in the language needed for formal academic learning, for abstract thinking, and for cognitively demanding tasks. Contrast **Basic Interpersonal Communication Skills (BICS)**.

cognitive classroom: A classroom in which the teacher emphasizes intellectual development rather than social or emotional development. See also **cognitive curriculum**.

cognitive coaching: The process of helping students gain an understanding of how they think and encouraging them to engage in metacognition, thus deepening their readiness to apply problem-solving and decision-making strategies. See also **metacognition**.

cognitive curriculum: A program of study that emphasizes academic achievement and learning over socialization and emotional development. See also **cognitive classroom**.

cognitive development: The brain's process, beginning at birth, of creating internal mental structures, or schemata, that enable thinking and learning. The cultures and backgrounds into which children are born affect what and how they learn. Children from enriched environments (in which parents and caregivers read to and with them, teach them letters and numbers, and take them to libraries and museums) come to school prepared to learn. However, some children arrive in school lacking most or all of these preschool advantages. The development of students' ability to think, read, reason, and learn is one of the primary goals of schooling. It is the job of the school to try to equalize the distribution of knowledge across society and to give students of disparate backgrounds and experiences a fair opportunity to develop their intellectual potential.

cognitive map: A belief structure, frame of reference, or mental representation that enables individuals to make sense of their environment as well as comprehend new ideas.

cognitive objective: The goal of study and learning, encompassing knowledge, comprehension, and synthesis. Contrast **affective objective**.

cognitive repertoire: The range of skills and strategies available to individuals as they encounter new information and new experiences and seek to understand them. The cognitive repertoire is a collection of internalized models of the world and strategies for operating on these models. For example, chess grandmasters are distinguished by having available for immediate recall a large repertoire of memories of particular configurations of chessboards, moves made in response to particular situations, and consequences of those moves. People with other experiences have different internal models of how the world works.

cohort: A particular group of students educated together. A cohort might be a group of students who started 9th grade at the same time, for example. Researchers might want to track such a cohort's progress through high school graduation to identify differences among students based on the courses they take or on other factors.

Coleman, James S. (1926–1995): A major figure in U.S. sociology and the study of U.S. education. For most of his career, he was on the faculty of the University of Chicago. Coleman was the lead author of the landmark report *Equality of Educational Opportunity* (1966), which influenced public policy about race and education for many years. For years, Coleman and others used this study to promote the busing of black and white students, but Coleman later revised his views on the value of busing and concluded that it contributed to white flight from urban schools, thus making desegregation more difficult to achieve. In his later studies, Coleman became an advocate of policies that were likely to increase families' social capital, including Catholic schools and vouchers. See also **busing; Coleman Report**.

Coleman Report: A major study, released in 1966, examining equality of educational opportunity in U.S. schools, looking specifically at the allocation of resources and the effectiveness of instruction in schools in relation to their racial composition. The report was written at the request of the U.S. Congress by a committee headed by sociologist James S. Coleman. Some commentators interpreted the report's findings to mean that "schools don't make a difference," because the amount of money spent seemed to have little effect on outcomes. Others interpreted it to mean that the racial composition and social composition of a school were more important than other factors—such as curriculum, instruction, and resources—in determining whether black students were successful. In this version, if a school was populated mainly by students from advantaged homes, their influence and aspirations would create a good learning climate for all students. On the basis of this latter reading, U.S. courts ordered involuntary integration of numerous school districts, in many cases involving the transfer of white and black students by bus to districts outside their own neighborhoods. Still others reviewing the report concluded that teachers' verbal skills were the most important factor in student achievement, regardless of students' race. Others argued that it would require more powerful changes—inside and outside the school—for a school to over-come disadvantages that accumulate during the time students are not in school. In the absence of definite conclusions about what must be done, the study was unable to predict which reforms would reduce educational inequality. See also **busing; Coleman, James S. (1926–1995)**.

collaborate: To work and play well with others, whether children or adults.

collaborative culture: An atmosphere of shared responsibility among teachers and administrators; also called a *democratic school community*.

collaborative team teaching (CTT): An instructional practice that pairs two teachers in the same classroom—one of them a teacher of general education, the other a teacher trained in special education—with the purpose of mainstreaming students with disabilities. As many as 40 percent of students in the classroom may have disabilities. *CTT* may also refer to any situation in which more than one qualified teacher is responsible for a given group of students.

collaborative writing: A teaching technique in which students work together to plan, draft, revise, and edit their written work.

collective bargaining: A process of negotiating a contract between an employer and its unionized employees—for example, between a school district and its teachers—to establish compensation scales, working conditions, schedules, and other rights and responsibilities.

college: A two- or four-year institution of higher learning that students enter after completing high school. Colleges offer a bachelor's degree after completion of a four-year course of study, either a Bachelor of Arts or a Bachelor of Science.

college admission requirements: The explicit expectations that a college describes for students who wish to be accepted—for example, a high school diploma, successful completion of courses in certain subjects, and a minimum score on a college admissions test, such as the SAT or the ACT.

College Board: An organization that sponsors the SAT, the United States' most widely used college admissions test. The College Board was founded in 1900 as the College Entrance Examination Board. Its goal was to offer a common examination for college admission that all students could take on the same day in different parts of the country. The standards for the examinations were created by teachers and professors of the academic subjects featured on the exams, and the exams were graded by teachers and professors of those subjects. The examinations—known to generations of students as "the Boards"—were essays or other written demonstrations of what the students knew. In 1941, with the outbreak of war in the Pacific, the leaders of the College Board dropped the written examinations and replaced them with the multiple-choice SAT for the sake of efficiency and speed. Today, the College Board is an organization that sponsors—but does not manage—college admissions testing; the managing function was turned over to the Educational Testing Service in 1947. See also **Educational Testing Service (ETS); SAT**.

collegial: An attitude of cooperation among professional associates.

Columbine: Columbine High School, in Jefferson County, Colorado, where on April 20, 1999, two youths murdered 12 students and a teacher, wounded 24 others, and then committed suicide. This shocking massacre spurred debate about gun control laws, high school cliques, bullying, and the effect of violent video games on adolescents. It also led to increased security in schools.

combat pay: Bonus pay for teachers who agree to teach in schools that other teachers avoid or want to leave, especially schools in very poor neighborhoods where there is poor discipline and low academic performance. See also **bonus pay**.

Comer School Development Program: A model school program that promotes collaboration among parents, educators, and the local community to improve the social, emotional, and academic outcomes for children. The program was founded in 1968 by Dr. James Comer, a child psychiatrist based at Yale University, who has written widely about child development and school reform. The Comer program, which has been adopted by more than 500 schools, uses consensus decision making, involves parents in school governance, and makes social and psychological services available to students and families.

common culture: The ideas, traditions, values, and experiences that unite the people of a society, regardless of their racial, ethnic, or religious differences. In the United States, Americans share a common culture that is shaped by laws, the Constitution, civic ideals, patriotic songs like "God Bless America," movies, sports, and an amalgam of shared cultural influences created by men and women of many different origins. In view of the great racial, ethnic, religious, and cultural diversity of the American people, controversies periodically erupt about the definition of the common culture. Ironically, such debates are themselves an essential part of the nation's common culture.

common schools: A term used in the 19th century to describe the first eight grades of public schools, which were supposed to be free and accessible to all the children of a town or city. In states where racial segregation was mandated by law or practice, the schools were not "common" to all children. But in New England, where the public schools originated, the common schools were there for all who wished to attend them. In the 19th century (and in some places even later), the high schools were not common schools because many charged fees or required students to pass entrance examinations. Most adolescents in the United States did not attend high school until the 1930s.

community-based organization (CBO): An agency that supports a public school's activities or receives a contract from the local school district to provide services to children and youths.

community-centered school: A school that opens its facilities and resources to the surrounding community to benefit people of all ages. The earliest example of a community-centered school was Benjamin Franklin High School in East Harlem, New York City, in the 1930s, where educator Leonard Covello opened the school for community use, provided adult education classes and summer school programs, became involved in programs to improve area housing and sanitation, and established community education centers in the neighborhood. The school no longer exists, having been replaced by a selective high school for science and mathematics.

community college: A two-year college, once referred to as a "junior college," that offers a wide variety of courses in occupational and vocational fields as well as regular programs in the liberal arts. Students in community colleges may earn an associate's degree or take non-credit-bearing courses. They can and often do transfer to four-year colleges to earn a regular bachelor's degree.

community empowerment: The act of giving people who live in the neighborhood of a school or who send their children to the school a sense that their views will be heard or that they can influence the actions or policies of the school.

community of readers: Students who read stories and books together in class. This phrase encompasses such activities as collaborative read-alouds, communal book reviewing, and other opportunities to discuss books with one's peers. See also **balanced literacy**.

community service: A term initially conceived to describe volunteer activity by adults and youths to help others in the local neighborhood but now referring also to required service, even to punishment meted out by the courts. The term once described the volunteer work of youth groups like the Girl Scouts and the Boy Scouts or religious organizations. More recently, however, community service has become a mandatory part of many high schools' programs. Students in these schools must complete a certain number of hours of community service as a requirement for high school graduation. Proponents believe that it provides a chance for adolescents to contribute to the larger society as well as a time for them to work alongside adults and learn about the adult world of work. See also **service learning**.

comparison/contrast chart: A graphic that shows the similarities and differences between two things or sets of things. Such a graphic could be as simple as a box divided into two parts—one labeled "similarities," and the other labeled "differences"—or two columns or rows with these labels.

competency tests: Tests administered by a school district or state that students must pass before graduating. These tests, usually multiple-choice, are sometimes called *minimum competency tests* because they do not require high levels of skill and seldom assess knowledge in any subject area other than basic mathematics and reading. Such tests are intended to ensure that graduates have reached minimal proficiency in basic skills.

competency trap: An overreliance on learning strategies that were previously successful but have ceased to be, or the belief that a problem was solved by a single approach when other factors were involved.

competitiveness: A reference to the increased demand in the world economy for educated and skilled workers, especially in technological industries. Leaders of business and higher education often refer to global competitiveness as a reason to improve the education and skills of the U.S. workforce.

composite score: The overall score on a test, determined by adding the scores on subtests—for example, the scores for reading speed, comprehension, and vocabulary on a reading achievement test.

comprehensible input: New knowledge that is only slightly beyond what the student already knows, so that it is not too far out of his or her grasp. This term is used in the context of second-language acquisition.

comprehension: Understanding what one reads, hears, or sees, a process usually involving the integration of new information with prior knowledge.

comprehension strategies: Any of a wide variety of techniques purported to help students understand what they read, hear, or otherwise observe. Examples of comprehension strategies include figuring out the meaning of words from context clues and making generalizations on the basis of specific facts.

comprehensive high school: A high school that offers a range of curricula, including an academic curriculum for the college-bound, vocational curricula for the work-bound, and a general curriculum for those who have neither college nor careers in sight.

comprehensive school reform: An approach to school improvement that involves adopting a design for organizing an entire school rather than using a hodgepodge of unrelated programs. During the administration of President Richard Nixon, the federal government awarded grants to school districts that promised to launch comprehensive school reform, a program that produced meager results since no one agreed on what constituted comprehensive school reform other than a promise by the district to be innovative. In the early 1990s, the administration of President George H. W. Bush encouraged the creation of a private agency, the New American Schools Development Corporation (NASDC), to promote comprehensive school reform. NASDC sponsored a design competition to find the best models for a "new American school." The federal Comprehensive School Reform Program, launched in 1998, described 17 models that the U.S. Congress recognized as research-based models; this program was subsequently included as part of the No Child Left Behind legislation in 2002. Since that time, many different school reform organizations have offered packaged versions of comprehensive school reform, all intended to change the culture of the school, create a seamless alignment between instruction and assessment, establish new and presumably higher academic standards, involve parents in the activities of the school, and sponsor better professional development than was previously available. See also **New American Schools Development Corporation (NASDC).**

compulsory schooling: Education that young people are required by law to receive (and governments to provide) up to a certain age, usually 16.

computer-assisted instruction (CAI): Educational programs delivered by means of computers and educational software. As computers have become more common in schools, the term and its abbreviation are used less frequently. In addition, CAI has specific connotations because it often applies to students with special needs. CAI applications include software programs and features designed to help students with dyslexia and poor fine motor skills; for blind students, Braille keyboards and the capability to display student work as synthesized speech or as a Braille display; and for students with physical disabilities, computers that can be operated by activating a switch by blinking or by moving the head, feet, mouth, or other parts of the body.

computer-literate: A term used to describe someone who knows how to use a computer; in the past, said of people who understood at least the basics of computer programming. As computers have become ubiquitous, instruction in the basics of computer programming has become relatively rare and less frequently included in computer literacy curricula.

computer-managed instruction (CMI): The use of software to record, analyze, and report on the outcomes of instruction. CMI systems are commonly used to report assessment statistics for individual students, classrooms, schools, and districts.

concept-based curriculum: A course of study organized around ideas rather than around a particular subject, era, set of facts, or set of procedures. Taken to the extreme, such an approach tends to deride the learning of "mere facts" as insignificant, compared with the study of large, overarching concepts.

conflict resolution instruction: Instruction that teaches students how to negotiate and resolve problems in a nonviolent way. Core concepts of such instruction include recognizing that there are alternative solutions to problems and learning skills to solve problems effectively. Conflict resolution is often provided through peer mediation, in which students assist other students in working through problems without resorting to violence. See also **peer mediation**.

consolidation: The act of combining two or more bordering elementary or high school districts to form a single district. The number of U.S. school districts has declined sharply since the middle of the 20th century due to consolidation of small districts: at the end of World War II, there were about 100,000 school districts in the United States; by 1990, that number had dwindled to 15,000.

constructed response: Written work by a student in response to a classroom assignment or a test question. An extended constructed response is an essay; a brief constructed response may be a few sentences or a paragraph in length.

constructed-response item: A test question that requires a student to give a written or an oral response rather than selecting a correct answer from a list of possible responses. Examples of constructed responses include a short written answer, a brief essay, or a demonstration showing how the student reached his or her solution. Some psychometricians prefer closed-response items, such as multiple-choice questions, because they are scored by machine and the results are therefore more reliable. Others, however, believe that constructed-response items are a better test of what students actually know and can do. See also **essay question; open-response item**. Contrast **closed-response item**.

construction of meaning: The act of thinking about ideas, events, and texts and ascribing significance to them. Those who use this phrase typically assert that texts are cultural products that do not have meaning in and of themselves; rather, the reader constructs their meaning, depending on his or her prior experiences and knowledge, his or her emotional state at the time of the reading, and the political and social climate in which he or she lives. Or, put another way, the text has no necessary relationship to what its author intended. This popular literary theory encourages readers to avoid seeking the author's purpose, since the author's purpose is allegedly irrelevant; it also encourages readers to believe that a text says whatever a reader thinks it does, which is a highly narcissistic, solipsistic notion. Teachers who act on this belief encourage students to believe that what they feel about a text is more important than the text itself.

constructivism: A philosophy of teaching based on the belief that students learn by constructing their own knowledge.

Constructivist methods center on exploration, hands-on experience, inquiry, self-paced learning, peer teaching, and discussion.
Constructivism is a direct lineal descendant of progressive education as espoused by John Dewey and his disciples, especially William Heard Kilpatrick. Constructivists suggest that only constructed
knowledge—knowledge that one works through oneself—is truly
integrated and understood. Proponents of constructivism maintain
that one learns best through a process of discovery in which there
is dissonance between old facts and ideas and new ones, which then
motivates the student to figure out new understandings. Critics of
constructivism say that this approach relies too much on student-
initiated inquiry, that it unfairly disparages the value of instruction,
and that constructivist methods place a heavy burden on teachers.
Constructivism is identified with inquiry learning, discovery learning, student-centered instruction, and other forms of learning in
which the teacher avoids or minimizes Direct Instruction. Contrast
instructivism.

constructivist classroom: A classroom in which the teacher uses
pedagogical methods that are based on the constructivist theory
of learning. The constructivist theory holds that the student is
the center of learning, and the teacher should act as a facilitator
of the student's learning, not as an instructor. The constructivist
classroom takes many forms, but at heart it is based on the belief
that the student is the one who does the learning and therefore
must take responsibility for his or her own learning.

content knowledge: Knowledge of ideas and facts in a particular field of study, such as history, science, literature, or mathematics.

content standards: Standards that describe what students
should know and be able to do in core academic subjects at each
grade level. In history, for example, content standards would
describe what students are expected to learn about specific historical events, figures, and ideas in each grade. In mathematics,
content standards would describe mathematical concepts and
skills that students should be introduced to at each grade level.
The purpose of content standards is to create a common curriculum, so that students who move from school to school or from
district to district have access to the same curriculum and so that

teachers know what they are supposed to teach. See also **perfor-mance standards**.

---

context-embedded language: Language supported by contextual clues, such as objects, pictures, and graphs. The use of this language facilitates instruction for second-language learners. When students talk to one another in the new language, they provide one another with context-embedded language that helps them grasp the meaning of words and phrases. Contrast **context-reduced language**.

---

context-reduced language: Language that lacks any contextual clues and is therefore abstract and difficult to learn. Written text that contains such language, without any clues of the language's meaning, presents barriers to second-language learners. Contrast **context-embedded language**.

---

continuing education: Educational programs offered by colleges, universities, and private-sector organizations to adults, usually not for credit toward a degree. See also **adult education**.

---

continuous progress: A system of education in which individuals or small groups of students go through a sequence of lessons at their own pace rather than at the pace of the entire class. Continuous progress has also been called *individualized education* or *individualized instruction* and is one version of *mastery learning*. In continuous progress programs, able and motivated students are not held back, and students begin new lessons only if they have the requisite skills. See also **mastery learning**.

---

contract schools: Schools that are operated under an agreement between a school district and an organization, either a nonprofit agency or a for-profit entity. The contract describes the expectations of the district and the responsibilities of the managing organization. It usually specifies a term of operation (e.g., five years) and may be revoked if the organization fails to meet its obligations to the district.

---

control group: In an experiment, the group that does not receive the experimental treatment. By comparing the control group with the experimental group, the experimenter can make an estimate of the effects of the experimental treatment.

controlled comparison: A statistical comparison between a treated group that receives a specific curriculum or teaching method and a control group to determine whether there is any difference in average performance between the groups. The comparison leads to an estimate of the treatment effect.

conventions of language: The generally agreed-on rules of grammar, syntax, spelling, and usage of a particular language.

conversion: The process of turning a regular public school into a charter school, either by the decision of central authorities or by a vote of the majority of parents and staff. In some cases, the conversion occurs as part of an effort to force change at a low-performing school; in other cases, the staff and parents want to remove the school from district control and seek the autonomy accorded by the state to charter schools.

cooperative discipline: Classroom strategies to deal with disruptive students through the use of praise, encouragement, and kindness rather than punishment or sanctions. Such an approach aims to build students' self-esteem and thereby get them to behave better and cooperate with others in the future.

cooperative learning: A teaching method in which students of differing abilities work together in groups on an assignment and receive a common grade. Each student has a specific responsibility within the group. Advocates believe that cooperative learning enables students to acquire both knowledge and social skills and that students try harder because they are members of a team. They also contend that students have more opportunities to ask questions and clarify confusions than they do in the whole-class setting. Critics complain that group work wastes time and that high-performing students end up doing most of the work.

coopetition: Collaboration among competitors. A combination of *cooperation* and *competition*, this term has migrated into the education world from the spheres of information technology and commerce. In education, it is often a euphemism for decisions made by planning agencies that intend to forestall competitive pressures or limit entry into a professional field.

co-op students: Students who spend part of their school day working in paid employment.

Copernican plan: A version of block scheduling, intended to rearrange the use of time in the school day so that students are in a single class for longer periods, class sizes are reduced, and teachers work with fewer students during the course of a day. This approach was developed in 1989 by Joseph Carroll, a school superintendent in Massachusetts; he named his plan for Copernicus because it was intended to bring about a revolution in educational thought, just as Copernicus had brought about a revolution in scientific thought. Advocates and critics differ as to whether these structural changes make any difference in what students learn. See also **block scheduling**.

core academics: The required subjects in middle and high schools, usually English language arts (reading, writing, and literature); history; mathematics; and science. In some schools, foreign language and the arts are included among the core academic subjects.

core curriculum: The body of knowledge that all students are expected to learn. High schools often require a core curriculum that may include, for example, four years of English, three years each of science and mathematics, two or three years of history, one or two years of a foreign language, and one year of civics and government studies. Nonrequired courses are called electives. In the 1930s and 1940s, the term *core curriculum* referred to a block-of-time program consisting of two or more class periods in which different subjects were merged into a single interdisciplinary program. Today, few schools have such programs, although interdisciplinary teaching survives, particularly in middle schools.

Core Knowledge (CK) program: A curriculum reform movement initiated by E. D. Hirsch Jr., based on his best-selling book *Cultural Literacy: What Every American Needs to Know.* Founded on the idea that there is a specific body of shared knowledge that all students and citizens need to know, the Core Knowledge program has developed a model curriculum from prekindergarten to 8th grade to show that it can be done. In his books, Hirsch urges school districts to offer a sequential, uniform curriculum that prescribes—on grounds of social equity—a significant portion of what students should learn about science, history, mathematics, literature, and the arts in each grade. Hirsch believes that such an approach will both raise the knowledge of the American people and help disadvantaged students, who often do not have access to the same knowledge as advantaged students. See also **cultural literacy**.

corporal punishment: Discipline imposed by striking a student's body with a paddle, one's hand, or some other instrument, with the intention of inflicting pain and humiliation. Corporal punishment was once commonplace in U.S. public schools, but it has been considered inappropriate, inhumane, and ineffective by most educators for many years. It is illegal in most states and school districts.

corrective action: A plan to improve low-performing schools, usually mandated by state or federal law or court order. Under the federal No Child Left Behind Act, when a school or school district does not make adequate yearly progress, the state must place it under a corrective action plan that includes resources to improve teaching, administration, or curriculum. If the school does not improve, then the state has increased authority to make any necessary additional changes to ensure improvement—for example, replacing all or most of the staff, contracting with a private entity to run the school, or reopening the school as a charter school.

Council for Basic Education (CBE): An organization founded in 1956 to advocate on behalf of liberal education and high standards in U.S. elementary and secondary schools. Its founders included some of the leading scholars and intellectual figures of the day, including Arthur Bestor, Clifton Fadiman, Mortimer Smith, and Jacques Barzun. CBE was a lively gadfly, puncturing pretentiousness and nonsense in U.S. education. The organization died in 2004, but the problems that it addressed did not.

Council of the Great City Schools: An organization based in Washington, D.C., that promotes the interests of urban schools through such actions as lobbying the U.S. Congress and issuing studies and reports.

Counts, George S. (1889–1974): A sociologist who was a leading authority on Soviet education and a prominent figure among Left-leaning progressives at Teachers College, Columbia University, in the 1930s. In 1932, Counts startled the world of progressive education when he gave a much-noted speech asking, "Dare the School Build a New Social Order?" He became a leader of those who thought that the school should build a new social order (they called themselves "social reconstructionists" and "frontier thinkers"), even if it involved indoctrination. From 1934 to 1937, he edited *The Social Frontier* (from which the "frontier thinkers" took their name), in which prominent writers debated political, social, and education reform. Although initially sympathetic to Soviet Communism, Counts turned sharply against it in the late 1930s. He was elected president of the American Federation of Teachers in 1939, where he opposed Communist efforts to infiltrate the union. His writings after World War II affirmed his strong support for American liberalism and democratic government.

coverage: The amount of time and attention devoted to specific topics in a textbook or a classroom. When there is too much coverage, teaching and learning will be shallow and superficial. The familiar complaint that teaching is "a mile wide and an inch deep" refers to the attempt by textbooks and state curricula to cram too many topics into a single semester or school year. For example, a one-year course in world history that "covers" everything from Plato to NATO is bound to be superficial and to provide inadequate time for thoughtful examination of important ideas. When coverage is too broad, students are not likely to absorb what they were taught. When coverage is limited to a reasonable number of topics, however, teachers have time to explain, to encourage class discussions, and to assign additional reading, writing, and projects. See also **a mile wide and an inch deep**.

cramming: Last-minute study for an examination.

creationism: The view that human beings were created by God out of nothing and did not evolve from other forms of animal life through the process of natural selection. Advocates of creationism believe that the creationist view should be taught alongside evolution in science classes. Opponents argue that creationism is a religious, not a scientific, position. They insist that the only ideas that should be taught in science classes are those that are based on scientific evidence and that are subject to rigorous scientific scrutiny. Courts have consistently refused to grant equal time to creationism on the grounds that it is a religious belief, not science. See also **evolution debate; intelligent design**.

credential: A state-issued license certifying that a teacher has completed the necessary basic training courses and passed the state teacher exam.

credit hour: A unit of measure representing the equivalent of an hour (usually 50 minutes) of instruction per week over a 15-week period in a semester or trimester system or a 10-week period in a quarter system. It is applied toward the total number of hours needed for completing the requirements for a degree, diploma, certificate, or other formal award.

credits: Points given to a student for successful completion of a course. Credits are usually based not only on passing examinations but also on completing a certain number of hours in class. High school students usually need a fixed number of credits to graduate.

Cristo Rey schools: A network of Roman Catholic high schools in poor urban areas. All students work part-time in entry-level jobs with local companies that in turn agree to support the schools.

criterion-referenced test (CRT): A test that measures a student's mastery of skills or concepts set forth in a list of criteria, typically a set of performance objectives or standards. Such tests are designed to measure how thoroughly a student has learned a particular body of knowledge without regard to how well other students have learned it. These tests may also have cut scores that determine whether a test taker has passed or failed the test or has basic, proficient, or advanced skills. Criterion-referenced tests, unlike norm-referenced assessments, are not created primarily to compare students with one another; rather, the goal is typically to have everyone attain a passing mark. Criterion-referenced tests are directly related to the curriculum of a particular school district or state and are scored according to fixed criteria. Contrast **norm-referenced test (NRT)**.

critical friend: A term used in professional development activities to describe someone who helps others by asking questions, reviewing their work, and enabling them to make difficult changes by providing regular, friendly criticism.

critical pedagogy: An effort by certain education professors to view schooling through a political lens, usually from a radical utopian perspective, with the hope of transforming education toward personal liberation or unleashing a social and political revolution.

critical thinking: The trained ability to think clearly and dispassionately. Critical thinking is logical thinking based on sound evidence, involving the ability to gather and analyze information and solve problems; it is the opposite of biased, sloppy thinking. A critical thinker can accurately and fairly explain a point of view that he or she does not agree with. Critical thinking requires close attention to facts, evidence, knowledge, and how knowledge is used, particularly in situations in which the facts are in conflict or the evidence permits more than one interpretation. This kind of reasoning is especially relevant for democratic life. Critics of the term think that educators have turned it into an empty cliché, since there is a tendency to refer to any sort of thinking as critical thinking.

Cuisenaire rods: Wooden sticks of varying lengths used in elementary classrooms to teach mathematical concepts. The rods vary from 1 to 10 centimeters in length and are colored so that each rod of the same length has the same color. Cuisenaire rods were introduced into classrooms as a means to demonstrate certain mathematical ideas—such as algebra—through physical modeling.

cultural literacy: Knowledge of the culture in which one lives—not only its vocabulary and idioms but also references to specific events, individuals, places, institutions, literature, myths, folk tales, advertising, and other "insider" information that would be familiar to those who have lived in the culture but that would be unknown to those who have not lived in the culture. It is the unstated, taken-for-granted knowledge necessary for reading comprehension and effective schooling within a culture. The concept of cultural literacy was popularized by E. D. Hirsch Jr. in his best-selling book *Cultural Literacy: What Every American Needs to Know*. Critics claimed that it was elitist for anyone to attempt to define what everyone should know, but Hirsch contended that the teaching of cultural literacy was egalitarian because it had the result of breaking down social barriers and disseminating elite knowledge to everyone. Further, describing what constitutes cultural literacy within a given culture is an empirical, descriptive procedure, not a prescriptive one. The cultural literacy needed in Brazil or France or Thailand, for example, would be distinctive to those who live in that country. See also **Core Knowledge (CK) program**.

culture of the school: The climate of a school, as defined by its traditions, celebrations, tone, values, ideals, expectations, sense of community, and usual ways of doing things. A school with a good culture has high expectations for student behavior, positive interactions between adults and students, a stable staff, positive school spirit, and good relations with parents and the local community.

curriculum: A description of what teachers are supposed to teach and students are supposed to learn in each course of study, often delineated for each grade. The curriculum describes *what* is taught but does not prescribe *how* that content is taught. So, for example, a curriculum for a 10th grade U.S. History course would list the topics and ideas that must be covered but would not tell teachers how to teach those topics and ideas. Scholars have added the following distinctions to the term: *intended curriculum* (what is supposed to be taught); *implemented curriculum* (what is actually taught); and *achieved curriculum* (what is actually learned).

curriculum framework: A grade-by-grade description of the curriculum that will be taught in a state's schools, from which the state's content standards are derived. Most states have curriculum frameworks in English language arts, history/social studies, mathematics, science, and other subjects. Some of these frameworks are so vague that it is hard to know what is taught in any given grade or over the course of 12 years of schooling; others are exemplary, specific descriptions that help teachers, parents, textbook companies, and assessment agencies determine what teachers will teach and what students are expected to learn.

curriculum map: A plan that shows how standards, frameworks, or state and district curricula are related to what goes on in particular classrooms on each day of the school year. So, for example, a state standards document might say, "Students will learn about various methods by which abolitionists opposed slavery (standard 1.E3a)," and a curriculum map might show that on days 33–36 of the school year, students in English 9 were reading *Narrative of the Life of Frederick Douglass, an American Slave*, or that on days 60 and 61, students in grade 7 U.S. History were studying the Fugitive Slave Acts and the *Dred Scott* decision. Each of these dates and classes would be associated with that standard.

curriculum of the home: What is "taught," more or less implicitly, by the home environment, which has a large influence on children's education. The curriculum of the home includes interactions between parents and children, including daily conversation; discussions of books, movies, and television programs; trips to the library or other community institutions; introduction to new vocabulary; and expressions of love. The curriculum of the home also involves daily and weekly routines established by parents for their children, such as a regular time and place for study and homework, play, and reading; limits on television watching or computer time; and family time for meals, hobbies, and activities. In addition, the curriculum of the home includes clearly communicated parental expectations—for example, that homework must be finished before watching television or playing games, that children must take responsibility for household chores, and that children must use correct and appropriate language. Parents also make it clear that they care about whom their children "hang out" with and about their children's academic progress, manners, health, and dress. If the curriculum of the home is successful, then children are likely to arrive at school ready to learn. See also **home environment**.

---

cut point: The dividing point on tests between different categories of scores; also known as *cut score*. For example, a score of 90–100 percent correct on a test is usually considered an *A*; 80–89 percent is a *B*; and so on. On the National Assessment of Educational Progress, independent reviewers determine the cut point that divides a student's performance of "below basic" from "basic," "basic" from "proficient," and "proficient" from "advanced." Cut points or cut scores are somewhat arbitrarily assigned; some states may set a very low cut point on examinations for science teachers so as to yield a large number of science teachers, or some may set a low cut point for end-of-course or graduation examinations so that few students fail to pass.

---

cyber schools: Education institutions that deliver instruction by computer via the Internet to students who may be at home or in charter schools.

---

cycles of writing: Repetitive efforts to produce a composition, going through planning, editing, and revision stages.

dance of the lemons: The administrative practice of repeatedly reassigning unsatisfactory teachers from one class or school to another, instead of going through a time-consuming effort to remove them through regular channels. Also known as the *turkey trot*.

D.A.R.E. (Drug Abuse Resistance Education): A drug education program that is extremely popular but of uncertain value. D.A.R.E. programs are in use in all 50 states and in more than half of all U.S. school districts. The program is taught by uniformed police officers, who aim to persuade students (mainly in the 5th and 6th grades) not to try drugs. The program was created in 1983 by the chief of police in Los Angeles, California, and has received strong support from law enforcement agencies, educators, and the media. Numerous evaluations have found that it has virtually no effect in preventing drug abuse, but it continues to enjoy widespread support.

data-based decision making: The process of making decisions about curriculum and instruction on the basis of statistical analysis of classroom data, school data (such as graduation rates, attendance, and dropout rates), and the results of standardized tests.

dead white men: American, British, or European writers and leaders, ancient or modern, who were presumably Caucasian and whose dominance in politics, science, or the arts allegedly crowds out the accomplishments of people who were not Caucasian. Criticism of "dead white men" is an implicit demand to pay more attention to others who were neither white nor men.

decentralization: The deliberate reassignment of decision-making authority from states or school districts to local schools or subdistricts based on the belief that those who are closest to a situation make better decisions and that people work hardest when implementing their own decisions. In 1969, after widespread protests in minority communities against centralization, New York City's school district of 1 million–plus students was decentralized into 32 community school districts; more than three decades later, in 2002, in response to low achievement and graduation rates, decentralization was abandoned for a centralized system of mayoral control. Site-based management, which transfers decision-making authority to individual schools, has cropped up as a more recent version of school decentralization. See also **site-based decision making (SBDM)**.

decision-making template: A term borrowed from industry and leadership training programs referring to steps one takes in making a decision. Some programs speak of a "five-phase decision-making template"; others substitute more or fewer phases or steps. Essentially, the term is just a fancy phrase to describe what one intends to do before deciding on a plan of action.

decoding: In phonics, the process of recognizing the letters that make up words and sentences, translating these letters into their corresponding sounds, blending the sounds to make words, and then understanding what the words mean. Phonics instruction is intended to help students "break the code" of the English language and become fluent readers.

deep understanding: The comprehension of what is taught in a meaningful way. Deep understanding is the goal of instruction; it is the opposite of superficial understanding, which often comes from studying material for a test and then forgetting it as soon as the test is over. Deep understanding means that the student remembers what he or she learned long after the course is concluded, although it is difficult to assess this outcome.

de facto segregation: Racial separation that occurs in a school or other public institution "in fact" or "in practice," as a result of such factors as housing patterns or school enrollment and not because of legal requirements. See also **de jure segregation**.

de jure segregation: Racial separation that occurs in a school or other public institution as a result of laws that require separate facilities for people of different races. De jure segregation was declared unconstitutional by the U.S. Supreme Court in 1954, in its *Brown v. Board of Education* decision. See also ***Brown v. Board of Education***; **de facto segregation**.

deschooling: A term coined by author Ivan Illich in his 1971 book *Deschooling Society*, in which he called for the disestablishment of institutions called schools. He emphasized instead the role of the community as the educator of the young. Many homeschooling parents admire the Illich philosophy of deschooling, believing that learning should be incidental, personal, and informal, detached entirely from any impersonal institutional structure.

desegregation: The act of eliminating racial segregation, whether the cause of the segregation is de jure or de facto. Efforts to increase the racial diversity of institutions, especially schools, may be the result of legal fiat—such as involuntary reassignment of students to different schools to maximize racial balance—or they may be voluntary programs, like METCO in suburban Boston. See also **de facto segregation; de jure segregation**.

detention: Involuntary detainment of a student, generally during what would otherwise be the student's free time, as a punishment for the student's misbehavior. See also **alternative instruction room; reflection room**.

detracking: The process of reducing or eliminating the practice of ability grouping, resulting in classes that contain students of all ability levels. In the past, tracking meant placing students in completely different programs—for example, the academic track, the vocational track, or the general track, so that a student's track determined his or her future career. The current version of tracking, in contrast, assigns students to specific courses with other students of comparable ability, with the best students in the top track and the weakest students in the bottom track. Grouping by ability for specific courses, such as mathematics, does not necessarily determine a student's career path, as the old-style tracking did. Yet advocates of detracking, also called *untracking*, point to research indicating that ability-grouped students in lower tracks don't get exposed to "high-status" knowledge. These advocates support detracking as part of a broader restructuring of schools aiming to group all classes heterogeneously and eliminate honors and advanced classes for top students. Critics of detracking say ability grouping is better for all students, both those who are academically gifted and should not be held back and those who are slower and need more attention paid to their special needs. See also **heterogeneous grouping**. Contrast **ability grouping; homogeneous grouping; tracking**.

developmental education: A euphemism on college campuses for remedial programs and courses, mainly in such basic skills as reading, writing, and mathematics.

developmentalism: The belief that students grow in accordance with their natural needs and that formal instruction should be delayed or minimized to avoid interfering with the student's natural development. This theory also holds that children learn only when they are ready to learn, both cognitively and emotionally, as determined by their stage of development on a presumed ladder of growth. Developmentalism began to gain prominence in the early decades of the 20th century when psychologists of education such as William Heard Kilpatrick advocated that the needs and interests of children should serve as their curriculum instead of academic subjects.

developmental lesson: A method of classroom instruction that begins with a motivational prompt (e.g., a cartoon, a newspaper headline, a brief reading, or an engaging story) intended to whet students' appetite for the information to be explored. The motivation leads directly to an instructional aim, which is the purpose of the lesson. The lesson progresses with a series of questions that elicit student responses to the teacher and, more important, to one another. This instructional strategy, also known as the *Socratic method*, requires the teacher to be prepared with a series of questions to engage and elicit student involvement.

developmentally appropriate practice: Curriculum and instruction that are suited to students' physical and mental development. Developmentally appropriate education is viewed as especially important for young children because their physical and mental growth rates vary widely and differ from child to child. For example, some 4-year-old children are able to sit quietly through group story time, whereas others become fidgety. Critics believe that the term *developmentally appropriate practice* has been misused by some educators to shield young children from any instruction, because they wrongly assume that the children are not "ready" to learn. Most teachers prefer to make decisions about children's readiness to learn based on observational cues.

developmental screening tests: Tests used to identify students' disabilities, including sensory impairments (e.g., nearsightedness or reduced hearing) and behavioral or developmental disabilities.

Dewey, John (1859–1962): The leading philosopher of U.S. education and the founding father of progressive education. Dewey was known to educators through his many writings and his emphasis on children's experiences as a source of learning. In his writings, he focused on the relation between how children learned and how they would later function as citizens of a democracy. Although Dewey was not opposed to teaching subject matter—indeed, the famous Dewey School at the University of Chicago featured a rich liberal arts curriculum in history, literature, and science—many of his followers interpreted his teachings to mean that *all* schooling should be informal and unstructured. Among Dewey's best-known books were *Democracy and Education*, *The Child and the Curriculum*, *The School and Society*, and *Experience and Education*. In the last-named book, Dewey chided the more extreme of his followers in the progressive education movement for thinking that subject matter could be jettisoned in favor of personal experience. See also **progressive education**.

diagnostic test: A test used to identify a student's specific areas of academic weakness or strength and, if possible, to suggest their cause. Often, such a test isolates specific parts of a body of information or skills, so that teachers can use the test results to understand what their students have mastered and what they have not. Such tests are deemed useful for instructional planning and are commonly prepared for basic subjects, like reading and mathematics.

diagramming sentences: A means of picturing the structure of a sentence by placing the words on a horizontal line that is divided in two. The subject goes on the left side of the line, and the verb goes on the right side. Adjectives, adverbs, and other parts of speech are placed on separate lines under the subject or verb in such a way that illustrates how they modify those words. Many students find that diagramming sentences is like a game and that it helps them understand how sentences are constructed, how the different parts of speech function, and why it is important to be thoughtful in placing adjectives and adverbs in a sentence.

Dick and Jane readers: A textbook series whose formal name was the Elson-Gray Readers, prepared by William S. Gray of the University of Chicago and introduced in 1930. The purpose of the books was to give beginning readers a simple vocabulary of easy words that they could recognize on sight. The readers were designed in keeping with the whole-word method of teaching reading, which was intended to replace phonics. The Dick and Jane readers were used by millions of U.S. schoolchildren and injected into popular culture such phrases as "Run, Spot, run." In the 1950s, a best-selling book titled *Why Johnny Can't Read* by Rudolf Flesch harshly criticized the banality of the books as well as their reliance on the whole-word method. In the 1960s, other critics charged that the Dick and Jane readers lacked any references to real life and were biased toward a world of white, middle-class, suburban, intact families. Despite the publisher's efforts to introduce nonwhite families into the books, the series eventually disappeared from the marketplace. See also **basal readers**.

differentiated instruction: A form of instruction that seeks to maximize each student's growth by recognizing that students have different ways of learning, different interests, and different ways of responding to instruction. In practice, it involves offering several different learning experiences in response to students' varied needs. Educators may vary learning activities and materials by difficulty, so as to challenge students at different readiness levels; by topic, in response to students' interests; and by students' preferred ways of learning or expressing themselves. Differentiated teaching assumes that classrooms will be grouped heterogeneously, mixing students of different levels of ability in the same class, although the strategy may also be used in classes for gifted students. Advocates of differentiated instruction say that it helps students progress by meeting their diverse, individual needs. Critics say that planning multiple learning experiences is time-consuming and that it requires extensive training. In addition, teachers of mixed-ability classes containing students of widely divergent abilities sometimes find the instructional burden to be overwhelming. Some parents of high-ability students in such classes complain that their children are neglected or not sufficiently challenged.

differentiated staffing: The school practice of having various instructional roles rather than a single role designated by the term *teacher*. In a school with differentiated staffing, various people play a part in the teaching process, but their responsibilities and pay may be greater or less than those of regular teachers. Typical roles include teacher aides, paraprofessionals (or assistant teachers), team leaders, lead teachers, and mentor teachers.

digital divide: The gap between those who have access to computers and those who do not. The term implies that the advance of new technologies creates additional inequity between haves and have-nots.

Direct Instruction (DI): Instruction in which the teacher explains the purpose of what will be taught and presents the content in a clear, orderly way, with students responding mainly to the teacher's questions. Developed by Siegfried Engelmann, Direct Instruction presents a strong contrast to inquiry, discovery, and constructivist methods, in which students are expected to develop their own ideas through investigation and discussion. Advocates of Direct Instruction say that it is more effective than constructivist methods. Critics contend that it is dull and dampens students' interest in learning. See also **systematic instruction**.

disadvantaged: A reference to students who lack favorable conditions for personal, social, and intellectual development, typically because of family poverty. Students from such backgrounds often have limited vocabularies and little access to academic knowledge in their home environment, and so begin school with disadvantages compared with students whose parents have a college education and a secure income.

disaggregation of data: The division of a body of data (such as the test scores for an entire student population) into segments (such as the test scores for given subgroups of students). Often, test data are disaggregated by economic status, race or ethnicity, gender, disability, migrant status, and first or primary language. Such data may reveal that certain subgroups of students are performing poorly in a school in which the majority of students are doing very well. Such disaggregation enables policymakers, public officials, parents, and teachers to see how each student group in a school or district is performing and to take appropriate steps to improve achievement.

discipline: (1) Punishment, as when a teacher finds it necessary to "discipline" a student for disruptive behavior in the classroom. (2) A field of study, such as the discipline of history or of physics. (3) Self-control, as when a person works to master his or her behavior and achieve a goal. (4) Training (by oneself, by teachers, or by an institution) that corrects or molds one's mental faculties or moral character. (5) Institutional rules that govern conduct and produce an orderly atmosphere.

discipline policy: The rules for acceptable behavior promulgated by school districts. Most educators believe that such rules should be clear and uniform and should specify the consequences for violating the rules. School rules usually cover such matters as bringing weapons to school, possessing or selling drugs or alcohol at school, assaulting a member of the staff or other students, fighting, committing robbery or arson, destroying school property, committing sexual harassment, gambling, plagiarizing, cheating on tests, forging notes from home, possessing pornography, and disrupting the classroom. The penalties for such actions range from moderate to severe, depending on the nature of the violation. For the least dangerous infractions, schools generally notify students' parents and ask them to meet with the teacher or the principal. Other penalties include detention (involuntary detainment during recess or lunch or after school); in-house suspension (assignment to special classes and isolation from one's peers); suspension (restriction from attending school for a certain number of days); police notification, when illegal acts are committed; involuntary transfer (reassignment to a different school); and, in the most extreme situations, expulsion. Most infractions of behavioral norms are dealt with informally by teachers and principals.

---

discovery learning: An approach to learning based on the principle of "learning by doing" in which new ideas develop. Discovery learning activities are designed so that students discover facts and principles themselves, through personal experience, rather than having them authoritatively explained by a textbook or a teacher. Discovery learning is prized by progressive and constructivist educators. Some of the principles of discovery learning have long been part of the repertoire of traditional teachers as well, especially in science classes, where, for example, students can directly observe the results of experiments. Critics claim that discovery learning is extremely time-consuming, difficult to manage, and inefficient because so much time is wasted waiting for students to "discover" what is already known by their teachers. See also **inquiry learning**.

---

disruptive student: A student who speaks out of turn or acts inappropriately with such frequency or intensity that it is difficult or impossible for the teacher to teach and for other students to learn.

---

distance learning (DL): The use of technology, especially television and computers, to offer classes in locations other than those where teachers present the lessons. Small high schools and rural schools may arrange for their students to take certain courses, such as physics or advanced foreign language classes, via television. Many colleges and universities broadcast or use the Internet to transmit credit courses to students who live in isolated locations or who for other reasons cannot attend classes on campus. See also **virtual schools**.

distracter: An incorrect answer choice to a multiple-choice item. For example, a test question may offer four possible answers (a, b, c, d), only one of which is correct. The remaining three incorrect answers are distracters. See also **foils; multiple-choice item; stem**.

distributed leadership: An agreement among staff members to rotate leadership and facilitation roles so that everyone fulfills his or her responsibility and everyone has a chance to have his or her professional needs met. Some refer to this consensus as a *flat hierarchy*, in which decisions are shared rather than made by one powerful person.

diverse providers model: A way of organizing a public school system so that some schools are managed by organizations that sign contracts with the school board. These contractors may be private managers, for-profit corporations, or nonprofit entities. They may contract to manage individual schools or to manage a group of schools. The conceptualization of this model is usually attributed to Paul Hill of the University of Washington. The model has been adopted by many large school districts.

diversity: Degree of variation in terms of race, ethnicity, gender, first language, disability, social class, sexual orientation, economic status, and other factors within a given group, such as a faculty or student body. Schools sometimes initiate programs or reforms to promote diversity or to increase understanding among different parts of the school population.

document-based assessment: Testing that relies on documents, typically authentic historical documents (e.g., old maps, letters, and passages from treaties, legislation, or court decisions). Students read the document and then respond to one or more questions about it.

document-based questioning (DBQ): A technique used both for instruction and for some state and national assessments that involves presenting students with historical documents and having them analyze and answer questions about them, either orally or in writing.

domain: A field or category—for example, the domain of knowledge or skills that might be assessed on a standardized test.

domain specification: A description of the range of knowledge and skills that will be included on a test or subtest or in a curriculum.

dress code: A well-defined set of rules about the clothing and hairstyles that school officials consider appropriate or inappropriate on school grounds. Some schools adopted dress codes or school uniforms because students were coming to school in clothing that was a distraction in an academic atmosphere; others were concerned that a certain style of clothing denoted gang membership. Girls were wearing skimpy clothing designed to display the maximum amount of flesh, and boys were wearing low-slung baggy pants that descended lower than their underwear. The rationale for dress codes is to establish a school atmosphere in which clothing is neither a status symbol nor a sexual provocation, and the focus is on learning rather than student dress.

drill and kill: A derogatory term denoting activities in the classroom that involve repetitive practice, the implication being that under certain circumstances such practice will "kill" student interest. Those who look down on repetitive practice tend to prefer inquiry learning, experiential learning, and other hands-on discovery activities. Of course, in any activity, a certain amount of practice is necessary to achieve proficiency in a skill; one rarely hears complaints about "drill and kill" from athletes, musicians, or dancers, for example. For educators, the questions are always how much of this practice they should engage in and at what point in the learning process, as well as which skills are best developed in this manner. Also called *skill and drill*.

drive: To cause forward motion or change by imposing a new set of conditions or incentives. For example, curriculum is supposed to "drive" instruction or assessment by describing what is to be taught and learned.

Drop Everything and Read (DEAR): A program that involves setting aside a regular time in the class schedule for independent reading. Students select their own books and are not expected to write about or otherwise report on what they have read. The program aims to get students to experience the joy of reading without feeling academic pressure.

dropout: A student who leaves school before graduating or receiving a diploma. Because it is difficult to keep track of adolescents who have left school, reported dropout rates are neither consistent nor accurate. For example, some students may reenter schools and drop out again more than once, and many students eventually get the equivalent of a diploma through the General Educational Development program. In addition, districts and states use a variety of methods to calculate their dropout rates, leaving the public confused about whether there is a problem and, if so, how serious it is.

dropout rate: The proportion of students who do not complete high school. There are a variety of ways to calculate the dropout rate, and school districts and state education departments can minimize or maximize the apparent problem by choosing from among different measures. For example, they may calculate the *event rate*, which is the percentage of students who drop out in a single year without completing high school; the *status rate*, which is the percentage of students in a given age range who have not finished high school or are not enrolled in school at a given point in time; or the *cohort rate*, which is the percentage of a single group of students who drop out over time. Status rates are higher than event rates because they reflect the number of students in a given age range who have dropped out of school over a number of years, rather than providing a snapshot of one year. Many researchers and policymakers agree that the best measure of the dropout rate is the proportion of all students who entered 9th grade but did not graduate from high school at the end of four years. This measure does not acknowledge that some students take five or six years to complete high school, but it has the virtue of consistency and clarity.

dual immersion: A program that offers instruction in both English and another language. Enrollees may include fluent speakers of English as well as native speakers of the second language. See also **bilingual education; immersion**.

---

dual language school: A school that teaches in two languages, alternating instruction between them so that students become fluent and literate in both languages.

---

dumbing down: The lowering of a curriculum's intellectual content and rigor. In a dumbed-down classroom, teachers may assign graphic novels instead of recognized literature; show students a movie version of a book instead of having the class read the book; inflate grades undeservedly; accept brief, shallow reports of only a few paragraphs instead of expecting thoughtful essays and research papers; rely solely on textbooks that have oversimplified content; and give full credit to sloppy, error ridden work.

---

dyslexia: A neurological learning disability characterized by difficulties with accurate or fluent word recognition and by poor spelling and decoding skills. These difficulties typically result from a deficit in the student's phonological component of language. Secondary consequences may include problems in reading comprehension and impeded growth of vocabulary and background knowledge. Dyslexia is the most common cause of reading, writing, and spelling difficulties and affects males and females nearly equally. The causes of dyslexia are neurobiological and genetic. With proper diagnosis, hard work, and support, students with dyslexia can succeed.

early childhood education: The education of young children, usually prekindergarten children.

Early College High School: (1) A program that enrolls at-risk and underserved students in an accelerated four-year program of study, beginning in 9th grade. The program is designed so that all students earn an associate's degree or 60 transferable college credits toward a bachelor's degree. Unlike *Middle College High Schools*, the Early College High Schools are not necessarily located on a college campus. (2) A program for highly motivated students with very strong academic skills who start college-level classes while they are in secondary school. See also **Middle College High School**.

early decision: A policy by some selective colleges to admit high school seniors in December of their senior year rather than waiting until the spring, which is the customary time for sending out admission notices. Early decision is only for students who have a clear first-choice college, because it's a contract between the student and the college: the student agrees that if he or she is accepted by the college, he or she will withdraw all other college applications and attend the early decision college. This policy lets students know sooner that they were accepted by the college of their choice while enabling the college to fill its freshman class with students of *its* choice. However, critics have long contended that early admission causes a loss of motivation among seniors who were accepted early and that it disadvantages minority students, students in rural areas, and other students who attend high schools with fewer resources. For these reasons, some selective colleges have abandoned this policy. Also called *early admission*.

Edison Schools: A private, for-profit company that contracts with local boards of education to manage public schools and charter schools. All Edison schools (named to commemorate inventor Thomas Edison) are expected to follow the company's model. Features of the model include extensive use of technology, individualized learning plans, teaching of values, encouragement of parent and community participation, and frequent assessment. Founded in 1992 by media entrepreneur Christopher Whittle, Edison is one of the most high-profile examples of private management of public schools.

edspeak: A language spoken by those inside the education profession. Edspeak is often not comprehensible to people outside the profession. The term is modeled on George Orwell's "newspeak" from his novel *1984*. Also known as *educationese*, *eduspeak*, and *pedagogese*.

educare: A term most often used generically to refer to developmentally appropriate preschool programs. The term has been widely adopted by commercial and private organizations to describe their early education programs. See also **developmentally appropriate practice**.

education: The purposeful, conscious effort to transmit ideas, knowledge, skills, habits, values, opinions, expectations, and standards through instruction, study, example, and experience. Education may be carried out in formal institutions, such as schools and universities, or in informal settings, such as families, book clubs, camps, and so on.

educational efficiency: A statistical measure used by social scientists to examine the ratio of educational outcomes (e.g., student achievement) to resource allocation (e.g., time on task, money spent, or number of teachers). So, for example, one might measure the number of hours spent on traditional grammar instruction against outcomes on the grammar portions of the Iowa Tests of Basic Skills. Or one might relate dollars spent on preschool programs to the high school graduation rates of students who have or have not attended such programs. Also called *educational productivity*.

educationally disadvantaged youth (EDY): Students whose families have a low income, as gauged by a federal standard; whose standardized test scores are below a certain point; or whose families live in a neighborhood with a low student graduation rate.

educational management organization (EMO): A private, usually for-profit organization or firm that establishes and operates multiple schools (often charter schools) according to a unified educational plan and management structure, often across district and sometimes across state lines. Among the best-known EMOs are Edison Schools, National Heritage Academies, and Victory Schools. See also **charter management organization (CMO)**.

Educational Testing Service (ETS): A nonprofit organization based in Princeton, New Jersey, that develops and administers a wide variety of tests to students and professionals. The SAT—a test of verbal and mathematical skills—is its premier product and is required by many colleges to gauge the academic readiness of applicants for admission. ETS was formed in 1947 by joint agreement of the American Council on Education, the Carnegie Foundation for the Advancement of Teaching, and the College Entrance Examination Board (now the College Board).

educationist: A professor of education. Usually a derogatory term.

Education Trust: An organization based in Washington, D.C., that advocates for school reform on behalf of poor and disadvantaged children. Led by Kati Haycock, the Education Trust has been a strong supporter of standards-based education.

educrat: A derogatory term, often found in tabloid headlines, to refer to a person who works in the education field, is fluent in edspeak, works in an education bureaucracy, and is not a classroom teacher.

effective schools: Schools in which all students, especially those from families in poverty, learn at a higher-than-expected level. The idea of effective schools was pioneered in the early 1980s by researcher Ronald Edmonds, who compared schools in which students of low socioeconomic status earned high test scores with other schools that had similar student populations but low test scores. He found that effective schools tended to have strong principals who closely monitored student achievement and created an orderly environment characterized by high expectations.

effort: Hard work; conscious exertion to reach a goal.

egg-crate school: Typical school architecture, in which each classroom is separated from the others, generally arrayed on opposite sides of a long corridor, and teachers work in isolation from one another.

Elementary and Secondary Education Act (ESEA): The principal federal law affecting K–12 education, first passed by the U.S. Congress in 1965 as part of President Lyndon B. Johnson's Great Society program. The law, which Congress is supposed to reauthorize every five years, was intended to improve the education of the country's poorest children, and that remains its overarching purpose. The No Child Left Behind Act of 2001 is the most recent reauthorization of ESEA and the most sweeping revision of the act since its creation: it vastly expanded the role of the federal government in public schools and districts throughout the United States, particularly in terms of assessment, accountability, and teacher quality. See also **No Child Left Behind Act (NCLB)**.

elementary school: A unit of schooling for young children, usually beginning in kindergarten or 1st grade and continuing through 5th or 6th grade. Instruction in the early grades of elementary school emphasizes the basic skills of reading, writing, and arithmetic while also teaching children such skills as how to cooperate in a group with others, how to work independently, and how to take care of themselves. These years are an ideal time to establish the foundation for later studies of science, history, the arts, and other subjects.

embedded questions: Guided reading questions that are placed within reading passages so that students can learn to ask themselves questions as they are reading. Such questions are supposed to model "active reading" and to teach students to think as they read. However, students may find it annoying and distracting to have their reading constantly interrupted by pedagogical activities.

emergent-level students: Students who are learning how to read but have not yet mastered the skills.

emotional intelligence (EI): A measure of an individual's ability to recognize and respond appropriately to his or her own emotions and to those of others. Some individuals suffer from neurological deficits, such as autism, that make it very difficult for them to recognize emotions in themselves or others. Some individuals with severe deficits in ordinary intelligence (for example, some people with Down syndrome) nonetheless have high emotional intelligence.

emotionally disabled (ED): A clinical diagnosis of feelings and behavior, such as anger, anxiety, or depression, that interfere with a student's ability to learn or participate in school activities.

empowerment: A transfer of authority from an official agency to others, such as parents or teachers. The term *empowerment* is used loosely; actual control over budgets and staffing is seldom relinquished by powerful government agencies to nongovernmental actors or even to governmental subunits. In some school systems, the term may refer to schools that are allowed greater flexibility to make decisions about curriculum, staffing, time use, and budget; however, assessment in these systems usually remains centralized, by either the school districts or the state (or both).

empty bucket approach: A derogatory way of describing teacher-led instruction, suggesting that children are empty vessels into which adults pour knowledge. Progressive—now constructivist—educators assert that people are active constructors of their own knowledge, continually reorganizing their understanding in response to new experiences. See also **banking theory of education; chalk and talk; drill and kill.**

English as a second language (ESL): Classes or support programs for students whose native language is not English. ESL classes generally have a stronger focus on English than do traditional bilingual programs, which emphasize students' native language.

English language arts (ELA): The academic subject previously known as English but now including such communication skills as reading, writing, speaking, listening, and viewing. The redefinition from *English* to *English language arts* shifted the subject's emphasis from the study of literature to the acquisition of skills. See also **language arts.**

English language learner (ELL): A student whose home language is not English and who has not yet acquired proficiency in English. See also **limited-English-proficient (LEP).**

English mainstreaming: The practice of placing English language learners in regular classrooms with the expectation that they will learn the language through frequent exposure to instruction in English and to other students who are using it. See also **bilingual education; immersion.**

enrollment: A count of the students enrolled in each school and district on a given day in the fall of the school year. This is a different figure from average daily attendance (ADA), which is the average number of students who attended school over the course of the year. The number of pupils enrolled in the school is usually larger than the ADA due to such factors as students moving, dropping out, or staying home because of illness. See also **average daily attendance (ADA).**

equality of educational opportunity: Equitable access to schooling, regardless of such factors as race, ethnicity, gender, disabilities, or socioeconomic status. According to this fundamental principle, schools are expected to provide a fair chance for all children to gain an education that will prepare them for full participation in U.S. society. This principle has been important in many court cases, particularly the U.S. Supreme Court's *Brown v. Board of Education* decision (1954). See also ***Brown v. Board of Education***.

equalization aid: Funds allocated on occasion by state legislatures to address perceived inequalities between schools and districts and to raise the funding level of school districts with lower revenue limits toward the statewide average on the basis of the size and type of district.

equity: Fairness. This term is often invoked by those who believe that government has an obligation to equalize students' access to educational opportunities, and thus their life chances. During the 1970s and 1980s, many state courts found great disparities in base per-pupil spending between high- and low-property-wealth districts. They mandated that these funding disparities be eradicated. In placing districts on a level playing field, the courts often invoked equal protection clauses in state constitutions. However, courts in many states have agreed with litigants that urban school districts should receive more than equal funding because they contain a disproportionate number of impoverished students and need extra resources.

E-rate: A federal program to subsidize Internet access and equipment for schools and libraries, included in the federal Telecommunications Act of 1996. E-rate allows schools and libraries to apply for discounts of 20 to 90 percent on local and long-distance phone and Internet access services.

essay question: An open-ended test question that requires a written response, usually at least a paragraph in length, in which the student can respond in his or her own words to the question. Advocates of good writing argue for essays that are far longer and that demonstrate understanding, knowledge, and skillful writing.

Essentialism: A movement that began in the late 1930s and was led by William C. Bagley, a leading teacher educator and educational psychologist at Teachers College, Columbia University. Essentialism emphasizes high-quality curriculum for all students, teachers as knowledgeable authorities in the classroom, and a strong teaching profession rooted in high-quality teacher education. Bagley and other Essentialists opposed progressive ideas, such as child-centered classrooms and the assertion that problem solving should replace academic subject matter. See also **Bagley, William Chandler (1874–1946).**

eugenics: A field concerned with limiting the reproductive capacity of persons presumed to be genetically inferior or unfit, with the intention of improving the human stock. When first developed in the late 19th and early 20th centuries, eugenics was considered a science devoted to improving the hereditary qualities of the human race by socially controlling the process of mating, akin to the breeding of plants or farm animals. Initially, it had broad support among prominent academicians and public figures. However, with the rise of the Nazi movement and its crude racialist policies, eugenics became a tainted field.

Eurocentrism: A perspective on the world that is centered on the history, cultures, and events of Europe. The term *Eurocentrism* is used to criticize accounts of history that pay more attention to Europe than to other continents or to reject a literary tradition that mainly emphasizes the works of European writers. It is not surprising that Europeans would be Eurocentric, or that Africans would be Afrocentric, or that South Americans would likewise pay attention to their own cultures and perspectives. But the issue becomes complicated when different cultures inhabit the same geographical space, as in the United States, where a European-dominated culture became aware of its many other cultures in the late 20th century. The challenge is to teach history and literature without falsification or boosterism. See also **Afrocentric education; multicultural education**.

Even Start: A federal program that provides grants to support family literacy projects, focused on low-income families. Even Start grants are supposed to incorporate early childhood education, adult literacy, parenting education, and interactive literacy activities between parents and children. Grants are usually awarded to government agencies, colleges and universities, public schools, Head Start programs, and public or private community groups.

evidence-based program: An educational program whose success has been demonstrated through sound evaluation or true experimental research—that is, the studies are based on random selection of participants and on random assignment of participants to different programs; are longitudinal (lasting at least three years); and result in long-term positive effects that are replicable. Critics maintain that the only evidence used to determine success is test scores and complain that other forms of achievement—such as graduation rates, persistence in college, and job success—should be taken into account.

evolution debate: Argument regarding the teaching of the evolutionary theory of natural selection, which is the basis of modern studies of biology. Critics of the concept, who call themselves creationists, oppose the teaching of natural selection in public schools unless the idea of creationism is also introduced as an alternative explanation of biological differences and, above all, the origins of humankind. Most scientists in the debate reject creationism as an expression of religious belief, and the courts have consistently agreed with the scientists. See also **creationism; intelligent design**.

exceptional-needs students: Students who have unusual or special requirements for schooling, including those who are gifted or disabled.

excluded students: Students who do not take a districtwide or statewide test because they are not proficient in English or because they have a disability. By purposefully excluding large numbers of these students, who tend to be low-scoring, a district or state can inflate its test scores.

exemplars: Samples of student work chosen to illustrate the level of academic work that is expected of students.

exhibitions: Demanding projects designed and conducted by high school seniors in schools that belong to the Coalition of

Essential Schools. Theodore Sizer, founder of the coalition, proposed the notion of exhibitions as an authentic way to assess students' learning in his book *Horace's Compromise*. Like other kinds of performance assessments, exhibitions cannot be used for high-stakes testing or for comparing schools or districts because they do not meet technical standards of reliability. Proponents of exhibitions argue that they are a legitimate alternative to standardized testing, referring, for example, to the judgments made when doctorates are awarded or when plays are performed. See also **Coalition of Essential Schools**.

exit examination: A test that a student must pass to graduate from high school. In some states, exit examinations are first offered in the 10th grade so that students have at least four or five chances to take them before completing their 12th year in school.

expenditures per pupil: The amount of money spent on education by a school district or the state, divided by the number of students enrolled.

experiential background: A student's life experience.

experiential learning: Education that emphasizes learning from firsthand, personal experiences rather than from lectures, books, and other secondhand sources. Experiential learning may take the form of internships, service learning, school-to-work programs, field studies, cross-cultural education, or training for leadership development.

experiment: A controlled test of a hypothesis in which an independent variable is manipulated for the purpose of observing its effects on one or more dependent variables. To conduct an experiment, the researcher or scientist needs to hold constant certain controlled variables so that he or she can isolate the effects of the independent variable. The difficulty of controlling for relevant (i.e., causative) variables is the primary reason that so much education research is unreliable. For example, an experiment in education might randomly assign students or teachers to various educational conditions, methods, or policies and then measure the outcome effects; in such an experiment, it is often difficult or impossible to know whether all of the relevant variables have been held constant. Sometimes such experiments are spoiled by teacher turnover or student mobility. Many education research experiments consist of trying something new and then observing the results of something different than usual. But without a control group and without randomized assignments to different treatments, an experiment has no scientific validity.

---

explicit grammar instruction: Instruction in the descriptive terminology and prescriptive rules of a given language, including syntax and the function of different parts of speech.

---

explicit instruction: Intentional, verbalized instruction in a particular concept or skill by the teacher, who stands or sits before the class, explains what he or she intends to teach, and then teaches it. Explicit instruction by the teacher is often accompanied by student practice of what was taught, either in the classroom or at home, and by evaluation of student work.

---

expulsion: The removal of a student from school because of unacceptable behavior that violates school rules. Students are usually entitled to a hearing and thus to due process before expulsion. Students who have been expelled are often permitted to return after a specified period of time. See also **discipline policy**.

---

extended-response item: A test question that requires students to write an answer of some length—longer than a single number, equation, word, phrase, or sentence—rather than to choose from an array of provided responses.

---

external examination: An examination conducted by an impartial outside agency or group. The National Assessment of Educational Progress is an external examination, conducted by agents of the federal government. Such an examination acts as an important independent check on the bias that occurs when local or state officials examine their own students (and therefore grade themselves). Other examples of external examinations include the assessment of a doctoral candidate's dissertation by a selected doctoral committee and the evaluation of a college's offerings and performance by a visiting accreditation committee.

extracurricular activities: Any activities that take place outside the regular academic program of the school or outside the regular school schedule, such as clubs, sports teams, or volunteer work.

extrinsic motivation: External rewards for excellent or improved performance or behavior, such as high grades and test scores, praise, school trophies and awards, school paraphernalia, money, treats, or the promise of getting into a good college. Contrast **intrinsic motivation**.

facilitation: The process of creating the circumstances in which something can take place, rather than taking direct action to make the thing occur.

facilitator of learning: A teacher who helps students construct their own knowledge rather than transmitting the knowledge directly to the students. The facilitation of learning is a concept drawn from constructivist pedagogy; the teacher is a guide and a "provider of resources" rather than the adult in the room who is responsible for instructing the students. In this role, the teacher de-emphasizes whole-class instruction, instead encouraging students to take an active role in their own learning.

factory model: A term used to describe a large, impersonal school in which there is no room for teacher creativity. Such a school tends to have a large and anonymous student body, tight supervision, time clocks, and standardization of teaching methods.

failing schools: Schools in which an unacceptably low proportion of students meet established standards, as compared with schools that have students with similar demographic profiles. See also **low-performing schools**. Contrast **high-performing schools**.

fairness: Lack of bias; said of tests whose questions are not weighted against any specific groups, such as females, minorities, or students of low socioeconomic status. Also said of tests that accurately reflect what students have been given a chance to learn in school. See also **reliability; validity**.

Fairtest: An organization that opposes standardized tests, both because of technical flaws in the tests themselves and because of the way in which test results are used (or misused) in rewarding students or denying them promotion or graduation.

family life education: School programs that teach the knowledge and attitudes that young people need to become responsible members of families, including knowledge about human sexuality and attitudes about appropriate behavior. Family life education programs are often controversial because one person's idea of proper values may be completely unacceptable to another person.

field trip: An excursion of school classes, led by school personnel, that may or may not have any relationship to the school's academic curriculum. Common destinations for field trips include museums, parks, zoos, science centers, manufacturing facilities, farms, and historic sites. Field trips encourage informal learning and are most effective when they provide experiences that support what students are learning in the classroom.

fishbone graph: A flow chart or diagram similar to the framework for diagramming sentences in English grammar.

fishbowl: A demonstration in class that uses students as examples. In teaching writing to a group of elementary school students, for example, a teacher may "fishbowl" a group of students conversing together about their lesson so that the rest of the class can see how their partnership works.

five Ws: The questions that must be answered when writing journalistic prose: *who, what, when, where,* and *why.* Together, the questions act as a formula for getting the basic story on an issue or a topic.

flagging: An action taken by a school district to review the enrollment records of a charter school and to freeze the charter school's public funding until the district's questions are resolved.

flexible grouping: Short-term grouping of students for various purposes, such as skill development. Teachers may group students by ability, interest, topic, or random assignment.

flexible scheduling: An approach to school scheduling in which classes are taught for different lengths of time on various days and may vary in size. For example, a lecture may be given to a large group for a relatively short time, whereas a seminar discussion would involve fewer students for a longer class period. Innovative secondary schools tried flexible scheduling in the late 1960s and 1970s, but few schools use it today. Also known as *modular scheduling* and *flexible modular scheduling.* See also **block scheduling**.

flip chart: A large pad of paper, generally placed on an easel, on which a person making a presentation to a group can write down the points that he or she wants to make. Throughout the session, the presenter can flip the pages of the chart to display information or to invite suggestions from the audience or class.

floor: The lowest level of performance measured by a test. Colloquially, the lowest score or ranking that a student can receive.

fluency: The ability to do a task automatically, without halting or pausing to think about it. For example, fluent musicians performing in concert know immediately which note or chord is appropriate at which time and do not need to stop to think about it; if they did, their performance would come to a halt. In reading, fluency is the ability to read rapidly with some specified level of decoding ability and comprehension. Fluency is the result of intensive practice.

fluent-English-proficient (FEP): Label applied to students who speak a foreign language at home but understand and communicate in English well enough to function independently in a mainstream English classroom. Contrast **limited-English-proficient (LEP)**.

fluent manner: Ease in carrying out an activity such as reading or speaking, with minimal halting.

fluent stage: The stage in the development of a student's reading ability at which he or she can read easily and well, without halting or pausing to figure out the phonetic code or to find out the meaning of a word. Decoding fluency is essential: without it, the student will not be able to read easily or well. Fluency in vocabulary and syntax is also important. Most important of all, however, is a wealth of basic background knowledge that enables the student to understand what he or she is reading without stumbling over its meaning.

focal skills: A method of teaching a new language that focuses on one skill at a time until students become competent in that skill. Students in such a program might begin, for example, with listening comprehension, so that they learn to hear and understand the new language; then move on to reading and draw on real-world material to build their vocabulary; and next, learn to write in the new language.

focus lesson: A lesson that a teacher in a balanced literacy classroom decides to teach on the spot on the basis of student discussion. In a focus lesson, the teacher typically discusses, explains, and demonstrates a strategy or procedure for learning, such as how to choose a book to read or how to listen to the group discussion. This kind of spontaneous action on the part of the teacher is widely considered an essential aspect of the balanced literacy approach. See also **balanced literacy**.

foils: The possible answers offered for an item on a multiple-choice test. See also **distracter; multiple-choice item; stem**.

foreign language study: The study of languages other than the predominant native tongue in a particular country or region. The study of non-English languages has a long and uneven history in U.S. schools. Until the 1920s, most students chose to study Latin as a foreign language. Although not a spoken language, Latin held high prestige because it was the language of scholarship and because the most selective colleges required Latin study for admission. Even students who had no intention of applying to an Ivy League school nonetheless studied Latin for two years in high school. It was believed that knowing the Latin roots of many English words would help students improve their English vocabulary and that the exactness and logical clarity of Latin "trained" the mind. German was also a popular foreign language in U.S. high schools until World War I, when many states banned the teaching of German. Foreign language enrollments experienced a long, steady decline for most of the 20th century. Recently, the study of Spanish has grown increasingly popular because of the proximity of Mexico to the United States and the presence of many Spanish-speaking immigrants in the United States. As the world economy becomes ever more interconnected, the study of foreign languages becomes ever more important.

form (of a test): A version of a standardized test that can be used interchangeably with other versions to avoid giving advantage to teachers or students who may have been exposed to a single form of the test. The various forms of a test are designed by psychometricians to have the same level of difficulty and to yield comparable results.

formative assessment: Any assessment used by educators to evaluate students' knowledge and understanding of particular content and then to adjust and plan further instructional practices accordingly to improve student achievement in that area. See also **summative assessment**.

formative evaluation: Evaluation carried out, often continuously or periodically, for the purpose of gathering information to improve student performance; teacher performance; and instructional methods, programs, and products. See also **summative evaluation**.

freak dancing: A sexually suggestive form of dancing, sometimes engaged in by adolescents at school dances. Characterized by inappropriate grinding, bumping, touching, and rubbing.

free appropriate public education (FAPE): Special education and related services provided to students with special needs at no cost to their parents. The federal courts and the U.S. Congress made FAPE a legal requirement for school districts and other public agencies after a long history in which many children with disabilities were not admitted to public schools and did not have equal opportunities for a free public education. See also **inclusion; mainstreaming**.

free school movement: A short-lived effort in the 1960s and 1970s to establish nontraditional schools that did not use textbooks, give tests, or have a prescribed curriculum. Many such schools were created outside the public school system, modeled on the example of Summerhill, the famous free school in Great Britain. They were intended to demonstrate that children could learn without incentives or sanctions and adhered to an extremely permissive version of progressive education. Such schools had antecedents in the early 20th century, including Marietta Johnson's School of Organic Education in Fairhope, Alabama, and Junius Meriam's Laboratory School at the University of Missouri. See also **Summerhill**.

Froebel, Friedrich (1782–1852): A pioneer educator and the founder of kindergarten. Froebel, a deeply religious man with a mystical temperament, studied with Swiss reformer Johann Pestalozzi, whose humane methods he admired. In 1837, Froebel opened a school for young children that he called the Child Nurture and Activity Institute; in 1840, he renamed it Kindergarten, literally a children's garden, where they could interact with nature and grow naturally, developing patterns of socialization and cooperation. The kindergarten had three parts: play with building blocks (which he called "gifts" and "occupations"); games, singing, and dancing for healthy activity; and observations of nature. See also **kindergarten; Pestalozzi, Johann Heinrich (1746–1827)**.

full inclusion program (FIP): A school program that places severely disabled students in regular education classrooms for the entire school day. Inclusion classes often require one or more special assistants to the classroom teacher. In a fully inclusive school or classroom, all the students follow the same schedules, and everyone participates in the same field trips, extracurricular activities, and assemblies. The Education for All Handicapped Children Act of 1975 (P.L. 94-142) required a "free appropriate public education" with related services for each child in the least restrictive environment possible and an Individualized Education Program for each qualifying child. In 1991, the bill was revised and renamed the Individuals with Disabilities Education Act. One related controversy involves interpreting the legislative phrase "least restrictive environment possible." Supporters of full inclusion interpret the phrase to mean full provision in the regular school, whereas others advocate case-by-case decisions, considering the needs of the individual student and the availability of staff and facilities. For example, some professionals and some parents of children with learning disabilities believe that some children benefit from partial inclusion, with a portion of their learning experiences occurring in alternative facilities using different teaching strategies. Advocates of full inclusion hold that all students are better served in structured inclusive classrooms and that children with disabilities receive more understanding and respect from their peers when they are in daily contact. Critics of full inclusion believe that the presence of many children with severe disabilities holds back average and gifted students and that students with special needs are frequently disruptive and are not well served by inclusion. See also **free appropriate public education (FAPE); Individuals with Disabilities Education Act (IDEA); least restrictive environment (LRE)**.

full-service schools: Organizations that provide services to both students and families—often including medical and dental services, nutrition classes, parenting programs, and social services —as part of the school program. Sometimes called *community center schools*, full-service schools provide essential services that many families could not otherwise obtain because of a lack of transportation, information, money, or time. Such programs aim to help parents feel comfortable with teachers, become a part of the learning community, and support their children's studies.

full-time equivalent (FTE): A statistical unit representing one individual attending school full-time. State and local funding formulas are often based on full-time equivalents.

functional illiteracy: The inability to read or write well enough to perform many necessary tasks in life, such as reading a train schedule, filling out a job application, reading a classified advertisement, or understanding a newspaper headline.

funding formula: An equation, usually devised by the federal or state education department, to determine how much money to distribute to public schools. The formula usually takes into account data for enrollment, attendance, the number of students with disabilities, the number of students who are low-income, the number of students who are English language learners, and a variety of other factors.

fuzzy math: A derogatory term used by critics to refer to new methods of teaching mathematics that emphasize estimation, multiple approaches to problem solving, and use of calculators in the elementary grades. These methods were recommended by the National Council of Teachers of Mathematics (NCTM) in its 1989 standards. Critics of fuzzy math, including some prominent professors of mathematics, believe that students should be expected to master such skills as adding, subtracting, multiplying, and dividing, as well as the fundamental algorithms and theorems of algebra and geometry. In the 2006 revision of its standards, NCTM restored the basic skills that had been de-emphasized in its 1989 statement. See also **Mathematically Correct; math wars; new math; new new math; whole math**.

gain score: The difference between a pre-test score and a post-test score; used as a measure of students' learning during a course of study.

gallery walk: A group discussion technique that checks on student understanding and teaches cooperative learning strategies. The teacher thinks up several questions and posts them in different sections of the classroom. Students are divided into teams of three to five and visit the different stations in turn, discussing and writing answers to the questions posted by the teacher. When the teacher says "Rotate," each team moves to the next station and begins a new discussion. Variations on this technique include the *gallery run*, with questions that require only short answers, and the *computer tour*, where the same tasks are completed on a computer. Teachers can use a *gallery walk rubric* to assess student performance.

gatekeeper: Any course or practice that a student must master to move to the next level of education. It is often said, for example, that algebra is a gatekeeping course because it determines students' access to higher education in mathematics.

gender bias: The unfair treatment of students of a given gender, intentionally or unintentionally, by school practices and expectations. The term may refer to expectations by school personnel that boys will have difficulty conforming to classroom routines or learning to read and write, or it may refer to subtle messages that lead to lower average achievement by girls in science, mathematics, and technology. The charge of bias is usually raised when test results consistently show that one gender is more successful than the other, as when girls persistently earn higher scores on reading tests or when boys persistently score higher on mathematics tests.

General Educational Development (GED) exam: The GED exam is a high school equivalency test that was first developed in 1942. Each year, approximately 800,000 adults receive a GED diploma—sometimes called an *equivalency certificate*—certifying that they have skills and knowledge equivalent to those of a high school graduate.

general track: A curriculum track, often found in comprehensive high schools, that is neither strongly academic nor vocational. The general program consists of a bare minimum of essential academic courses in mathematics, English, social studies, and general science but is not a college-preparatory program; it may include a few vocationally oriented courses, but it does not lead to mastery of any vocational skills. It has generally been populated by students with no particular interest in higher education who are looking for the easiest way to get a high school diploma. By the 1970s, a plurality of high school students were enrolled in the general track, but this proportion declined after the 1983 report *A Nation at Risk* called on high schools to expect all students to complete a basic curriculum that included four years of English, three years of math and science, and three years of social studies.

generative thinking: Cogitation that goes beyond whatever the student has memorized or been taught. For example, original writing requires generative thinking.

genre study: In reading and literature classes, the study of a particular type or form of writing, such as biography, short story, novel, oration, essay, lyric poetry, epic poetry, tragedy, comedy, or farce.

Gifted and Talented Education (GATE): A program offered in some districts or schools to benefit students who have been identified by tests or other measures as unusually intelligent or talented. Traditionally, gifted students were selected on the basis of intelligence test results. However, a revolt against intelligence tests and any other measures limited solely to intellectual qualities broadened the definition of *giftedness* to include students who are deemed to have other kinds of potential or who evince talent in such areas as leadership or the visual and performing arts. In some districts or schools, gifted programs have been defined as enrichment activities that are appropriate for all students; such programs presume that all students are gifted. Programs for students of unusual intellectual caliber have never enjoyed broad popular support, and efforts to give these students an education that challenges them are often considered elitist.

global studies: An academic program devoted to the study of the histories, cultures, geography, economies, and governments of the nations of the world. Unlike world history, global studies tends to emphasize the study of cultures over the study of political history and struggles for power between and within nations.

goal-oriented: A description of organizations or individuals with a clear focus and mission.

goal setting: The process of setting specific, measurable objectives to work toward, with a defined end point.

grade: (1) A judgment on student performance or conduct, rendered usually either as a letter from *A* to *F* (with *A* representing excellence and *F* representing failure) or as a number, generally from 0 to 100, with 100 representing a perfect performance. Teachers may award grades for test performance, classroom participation, homework, or other student work. (2) A level of education attainment, ranging from grade 1 to grade 12.

grade configuration: Decisions about which grade levels belong in which schools. One pattern places students from kindergarten to 6th grade in elementary school, students from 7th through 9th grade in junior high school, and students from 10th through 12th grade in high school. However, many districts prefer to place K–5 students in elementary school, students in grades 6–8 in middle school, and students in grades 9–12 in high school. Others favor a K–8 and 9–12 arrangement. There is no set pattern that is accepted everywhere, and grade configuration can sometimes become a topic of heated debate—for example, between supporters and critics of middle school.

grade inflation: The practice by teachers and professors of awarding grades that are higher than the students' work deserves. The reasons for grade inflation are many: a general downward drift in standards, the desire of teachers to be popular with students or to get a good rating on students' evaluations, or the belief of teachers that too many students would fail if grades accurately reflected the quality of their work.

grade level: (1) A student's placement in school (e.g., 4th grade), not counting kindergarten or preschool. (2) The difficulty level of curriculum and test content designed for typical students in a given year of school. If a given book, software program, or instructional strategy, for example, is appropriate for the average student in a particular grade, it is said to be on grade level. When used in the context of testing, the term can be confusing. If the test is normed, then half of the students will always be above grade level and half below. If the test is standards-based, however, the term *grade level* is inapplicable because the results show which proportion of students met the standards, not whether they are at grade level.

grade-level expectation: An objective that states a goal or benchmark that students are expected to meet at a particular grade level in a particular subject.

grade point average (GPA): The average of a student's grades over a set period of time, such as the four years of high school. The GPA is used to establish class ranking and is often a significant determinant of college admission.

grade reform: Any change in the method by which a student's academic progress is reported to the student, parents, and others. A common elementary-level grade reform is to replace traditional letter grades with narrative reports that describe the student's progress toward a set of goals.

grading on the curve: A grading technique that assigns grades in such a manner as to approximate a normal, or bell curve, distribution. If the sample size is large enough, then most analyses of human characteristics or performance tend to fall naturally into a regular, bell-shaped pattern, with most people lumped toward the middle and outliers at either end. Grading on a curve assumes that grades should follow this bell-shaped pattern, with a few students getting *F*s, a few getting *A*s, and most somewhere in the middle, getting *C*s. So, for example, the top 10 percent should get *A*s, the next 20 percent below that *B*s, the 40 percent in the middle *C*s, and so on. Essentially, grading on a curve involves assigning marks for the quality of students' work relative to one another rather than on the basis of a specified mastery criterion. When grading on the curve, a teacher will always assign the best paper or test an *A* and the worst an *F*, and all other papers or tests will be arrayed between them. In contrast, if the criterion were mastery of the content, it is theoretically possible that even the "worst" paper or test might earn a passing mark. Critics of grading on the curve say that it depresses student motivation, since many students know they will never succeed. See also **bell curve; normal curve**.

graduation requirements: The courses and activities that a high school or a school district establishes as necessary for a student to complete to receive a high school diploma.

grain size: The specificity of information—for example, whether the data refer to a nation, a state, a city, a local district, a school, a group of students, a class, or a student.

grammar: The set of rules governing the use of a language, including knowledge of the parts of speech and of correct syntax. Knowledge of grammar enables one to communicate effectively—to say and write what one means with clarity, accuracy, and coherence. Linguists often distinguish between this kind of rules-based grammar and grammar as it occurs in the usage shared by a community of speakers. It is useful to know both kinds, so that one may participate in the public sphere, where formal rules matter, and in one's private sphere, where personal communications may depend more on idioms and nonverbal exchanges than on formal accuracy of expression.

grammar of schooling: The assumption that schools have certain invariable features, such as classrooms, teachers, subjects, textbooks, tests, report cards, rewards and sanctions, a certain architecture, and a certain layout of the classroom. Education historians David Tyack and William Tobin are credited with the phrase and the observation that the grammar of schooling is remarkably resistant to change.

graphic novels: Long-form works in comic book form, often with complex storylines. Some educators prefer using graphic novels rather than traditional novels to promote literacy because they are easier to read and show the action in drawings. Advocates say that anything that gets students to read is worthy, but critics say that graphic novels contribute to the dumbing down of the curriculum and that they are no replacement for real literature.

graphic organizer: Any chart, graph, table, drawing, or other graphic device that is used for brainstorming, organizing ideas, or planning. Examples of graphic organizers include story maps, word webs or cluster charts, Venn diagrams, tree diagrams, flowcharts, matrices, comparison/contrast charts, cause-and-effect charts, problem/solution charts, histograms, pie charts, and line graphs.

graphophonic cues: Hints based on sound-symbol correspondences that help readers decode and comprehend a text.

Great Books program: A course of study based on reading and discussion of certain classic writings. The Great Books program was created at the University of Chicago in the 1930s by philosopher Mortimer Adler and university president Robert Maynard Hutchins. With the assistance of a distinguished editorial board, they designated specific works of literature, history, philosophy, government, mathematics, and science as the "great books" of Western civilization. The Great Books became an important part of studies at the University of Chicago, Columbia University, St. John's College, and the University of Virginia, as well as of honors programs at various other institutions and of informal adult study groups. A junior version of the Great Books program was later created for junior high and high school students. See also **Adler, Mortimer J. (1902–2001); Hutchins, Robert Maynard (1899–1977).**

gridded-response question: A question on a standardized test requiring students to solve a problem with a numerical answer and then to record that answer both by writing the number in the blank space provided and by filling in bubbles corresponding to that number on a grid.

group intelligence tests: Tests designed to screen a large number of people quickly to determine which have the highest levels of intelligence. Such tests were first created by leading U.S. psychologists during World War I to screen thousands of military recruits and identify those who should be selected for training as officers. Psychologists such as Robert Yerkes of Harvard University, Lewis Terman of Stanford University, Carl C. Brigham of Princeton University, and Edward L. Thorndike of Teachers College, Columbia University, designed these tests, which they believed were able to put a precise number on "innate" intelligence. After the war, the tests were redesigned for use in the public schools to assess students' intelligence and to tailor instruction to students' presumed aptitude. For many years, the tests were used as important tools in identifying gifted students and assigning students to different programs.

guidance counselor: A school official who helps students deal with their personal and social problems and advises them in planning for their futures after high school graduation, whether they plan to attend college or join the workforce.

guided reading groups: Groups of students, often organized by ability level, that an instructor or facilitator leads in guided reading instruction.

guided reading instruction: A method of reading instruction in which the instructor walks one or more students (often students in a small group, or *literacy circle*) through a text, reading it aloud and pausing from time to time to engage the student or students in thinking about aspects of the text. Guided reading often involves instruction in specific reciprocal learning strategies, including summarizing, predicting, questioning, and clarifying. Many textbooks now include guided reading questions in their study apparatus. Proponents of guided reading say that students need direction to concentrate on what is important, but critics contend that emphasis on skills rather than content defers students' acquisition of background knowledge, which is essential for comprehension.

guided writing: A teaching technique in which the teacher encourages students to write, to revise, and to think about how to improve their writing by walking them step-by-step through the requirements of the writing process. Critics of guided writing say that it is too routinized and technical and that it dampens spontaneity and creativity.

guide on the side: The teacher as a facilitator of learning, not someone who instructs students directly; the ideal educator, according to the expression, "A teacher should be a guide on the side, not a sage on the stage." Contrast **sage on the stage**.

habits of mind: The ways in which students should think as they learn. The phrase was popularized in the 1980s by Theodore Sizer of the Coalition of Essential Schools and Deborah Meier of Central Park East Secondary School. Sizer writes about eight habits of mind, including perspective, analysis, imagination, empathy, communication, commitment, humility, and joy. Meier writes of the habits of mind as a series of five questions, including "How do we know what we know?"; "Who's speaking?"; "What causes what?"; "How might things have been different?"; and "Who cares?" The purpose of those who advocate habits of mind is to direct attention to how students learn to think, rather than create a laundry list of what they should know. Habits of mind are not, however, a substitute for a curriculum organized around subject matter. Educators such as Robert Maynard Hutchins and Mortimer Adler at the University of Chicago used the phrase *habits of mind* during the 1930s and 1940s to stress the value of studying the Great Books.

hands-on activities: Activities, often "real-world" tasks, that engage students' physical skills to solve problems.

handwriting: Penmanship; the skill of writing legibly using a pen or pencil. Handwriting was once taught intensively in U.S. elementary schools, where students practiced their handwriting by the hour, trying to demonstrate that they could write their words, sentences, paragraphs, and essays in a clean and clear style. Today, with the widespread availability of computers, it is generally assumed that handwriting has become obsolete. However, handwriting continues to be important in many matters, such as writing medical prescriptions, copying phone numbers, addressing letters and packages, and filing tax returns. Errors in any of these instances can be extremely costly to individuals and to society, yet can be easily avoided by ensuring that every high school graduate can write legibly.

hard-to-staff schools: Low-performing schools that have difficulty recruiting and retaining teachers because of poor working conditions. A number of conditions can make a school hard to staff: it may have poor leadership, experience high student turnover, have poor student discipline, or be in a neighborhood where teachers feel unsafe, for example. In some districts, teachers are paid a bonus to work in these schools. See also **combat pay; low-performing schools**.

Harris, William Torrey (1835–1909): A major figure in the history of U.S. education and a champion of liberal education for all children. As superintendent of schools in St. Louis, Missouri, Harris established the United States' first permanent kindergarten. He was also a leading scholar of Hegel and edited philosophical journals. In 1889, President Benjamin Harrison appointed him as U.S. Commissioner of Education, in which capacity he served for 18 years. Harris was a tireless reformer who advocated on behalf of universal public education, a modern curriculum, and schools that teach every youngster "versatile intelligence," self-control, and "the art of intellectual self-help."

Head Start: A federal program of preschool education for children from low-income families, established in 1965 as part of the government's War on Poverty. Head Start began as an eight-week summer program and eventually became a full-year program offering a wide range of services, including medical, social, psychological, and nutritional components. The program has enjoyed broad popular support, although critics contend that it pays too little attention to preparing children for literacy and numeracy. See also **prekindergarten**.

---

helicopter parents: A description of parents who hover over their children and become intensely involved in every aspect of their lives. Such parents pester college counselors, complain to teachers about their children's grades, and otherwise attempt to protect their children from any setbacks. Parents whose zeal causes them to engage in unethical behavior, such as completing their children's homework or writing their college application essays, are called "Black Hawks," after the combat helicopters of the same name.

Herbart, Johann Friedrich (1776–1841): A founder of modern scientific pedagogy who taught psychology and philosophy in German universities and whose writings influenced the theory and practice of education in Europe and the United States. In opposition to the then-popular belief that the mind consisted of a series of muscles that need to be trained and exercised, Herbart held that student interest develops as new ideas are linked sequentially to preexisting knowledge. Teacher training institutions on both sides of the Atlantic adopted methods based on Herbartian ideas. In its most common form, the Herbartian approach involved five steps: preparing the pupils for a new lesson, presenting the lesson, associating the new lesson with ideas previously studied, generalizing the lesson's major points, and applying the lesson (or, in some versions, testing pupils to see whether they had learned the lesson). Following Herbartian ideas about correlation and concentration of studies, his U.S. disciples emphasized history and literature as the heart of the curriculum in the elementary grades. Herbart's ideas were swept aside in the early 20th century by advocates of child-centered education.

---

heredity versus environment: A long-running debate about whether individuals are influenced more by their heredity (their genetic makeup) or by their environment (the circumstances in which they grow up). Also referred to as *nature versus nurture*.

heterogeneous grouping: The practice of assigning students to a class without regard to their tested ability. See also **detracking**. Contrast **ability grouping; homogeneous grouping; tracking**.

heuristic: A rule of thumb or procedure that works to provide a satisfactory if not optimal solution to a problem; a technique of discovery, invention, and problem solving through experimental or trial-and-error techniques. Some examples of heuristics include throwing out parts of a problem and solving the simplified version; breaking a problem into parts and solving each one separately; and means-ends analysis—defining the current situation, describing the end state, and then taking steps to reduce the differences between them.

hidden curriculum: What schools teach students by example and by their social organization, as opposed to the subject matter that they officially teach. For example, a school's hidden curriculum might teach that boys are strong and undisciplined and girls are smart and well behaved; or that learning is something that is done to students rather than something that students must do for themselves; or that being popular is more important than being smart; or that societies are organized according to rules, that some of these rules are arbitrary, and that there are consequences for breaking the rules. Some of the hidden curriculum is good, and some of it is not. Some of what sociologists call the hidden curriculum is due not to socialization but to human nature. Like other large social organizations, schools need rules to function, and people need to learn what the rules are, when to follow them, and when it is appropriate to challenge them.

higher-order thinking skills (HOTS): Sophisticated cognitive abilities, including the ability to understand complex concepts, to compare and contrast different opinions, or to apply conflicting information to the solution of a problem that has more than one answer. Although such skills are highly praised today—and indeed, often prized above content knowledge—they cannot be attained without also gaining mastery of a significant amount of knowledge to think critically about.

highly qualified teachers (HQTs): According to the No Child Left Behind legislation, teachers who have obtained full state teacher certification or licensure, hold a minimum of a bachelor's degree, and have demonstrated that they know each of the academic subjects they teach. They can meet the last requirement by having a graduate degree in the subject, majoring in the subject, earning enough credits to constitute a major, or passing a test of the subject. Current teachers may be deemed qualified if they successfully go through a process known as HOUSSE (High, Objective, Uniform State Standard of Evaluation), which takes into account years of experience or participation in workshops. See also **HOUSSE (High, Objective, Uniform State Standard of Evaluation)**.

high-performing schools: Schools whose students consistently earn higher-than-average test scores, as compared with schools with similar demographics. Different states and private organizations vary in their definitions of high-performing schools. By some definitions, for example, the top 25 percent of schools in a state or district are high-performing; according to other definitions, high-performing schools are those that consistently show higher-than-expected test scores for black students, Hispanic students, low-income students, and/or students with special needs. Contrast **failing schools; low-performing schools**.

high school: An academic institution that may include grades 9–12 or grades 10–12. It is the final segment of compulsory secondary education in students' educational experience before they decide whether to continue to postsecondary education, to enter the workforce, to join the military, to be a parent, or to take some other path.

high school competency tests: Tests that assess student attainment of the minimal level of knowledge and skills required to obtain a high school diploma. A high school competency test generally assesses basic skills in such areas as reading, writing, and mathematics. See also **competency tests**.

high-stakes test: A criterion-referenced test that results in serious consequences for those who score low and/or some kind of reward for those who score high. For example, students who pass a high school exit exam typically receive a diploma, whereas students who fail the exam do not receive one. Another example of a high-stakes test is one that determines whether a student is promoted to the next grade in school. Contrast **low-stakes test; no-stakes test**.

---

holistic education: Education that focuses on the *whole* child, not just on the child's growth in cognitive skills and knowledge. From a holistic perspective, teachers must draw from both the cognitive and the affective domains and attend to students' physical health, emotional well-being, and social interactions with others. In some schools devoted to holistic education, these concerns are given higher priority than cognitive skills and knowledge. Critics point out, however, that schools cannot meet every need equally and that teachers cannot take the place of parents and social workers. See also **meeting the needs of the whole child**.

---

holistic evaluation: The assignment of a single score based not on an item-by-item analysis but on the evaluator's judgment of the overall quality of the student's work. For example, a holistic evaluation of a test would attach little importance to the test taker's grammatical, spelling, or even factual errors, but rather would be based on the overall quality of the student's response on the test. Critics of holistic evaluation claim that it is too subjective, as compared with other kinds of scoring, and that it devalues important skills such as accuracy of expression.

---

holistic thinking: The thinking that occurs when students perform complex tasks connected to real-world situations requiring problem solving, decision making, collaboration, and the use of tools and technology. Efforts to foster holistic thinking are usually contrasted with instruction that teaches discrete skills or emphasizes the acquisition of knowledge. The pursuit of holistic thinking often leads to interdisciplinary courses and the presentation of real-world problems without disciplinary boundaries. There is no research, however, to show that holistic thinking emerges from holistic problems. Although the world may be a seamless whole with all its parts interrelated, the ability to think clearly about those interrelationships requires a solid foundation of skills and knowledge in known disciplines of thinking. Many of the world's eminent holistic thinkers, like John Dewey, did not receive a holistic education.

---

home environment: The social, emotional, and physical circumstances in a student's home. The student's home environment includes, for example, the degree of nurturing and care provided by his or her family; the availability of books, magazines, and newspapers; the presence or absence of a regular place to study and of time set aside for study; and the extent to which responsible adults monitor the student's behavior, establish clear expectations, limit television watching and computer games, and make sure that the student's peer group has good values. See also **curriculum of the home**.

home language: The language that a student speaks at home with his or her family.

homeroom: A period in a secondary school, usually at the beginning of the day, when a teacher meets with a small group of students. Sometimes also called *Achievement Time* or *Time to Care*. See also **advisory**.

homeschooling: The education of students at home rather than in a public or private school. In the early years of the 21st century, more than 1 million children were homeschooled. Parents have many reasons for making the decision to teach their children at home, but the common thread is that they believe it will be in the best interest of their children. Often, parents choose to homeschool their children to keep them from exposure to what they consider to be the corrupting influences within schools, such as the availability of drugs or alcohol, sexual permissiveness among peers, or challenges to religious beliefs. Homeschooling families often join together in networks to share resources and ideas, and they use the Internet extensively.

homework: School assignments that must be completed outside class, usually at home. Homework teaches students to complete assignments independently, without the immediate supervision of a teacher. It also extends the amount of time available for learning. Although numerous books and articles have denounced homework, the reality is that this is often the only way students have time to read a book, write an essay, conduct research for a project, or practice problem-solving activities.

homogeneous grouping: The practice of assigning students to a class on the basis of their ability, usually ascertained through testing, with all students in the class performing at similar levels. For example, homogeneous grouping may separate students into regular, advanced, and remedial classes. See also **ability grouping; tracking**. Contrast **detracking; heterogeneous grouping**.

---

honors track: A program of studies in high school designed for high-achieving students who are qualified to take rigorous and advanced academic courses.

HOUSSE (High, Objective, Uniform State Standard of Evaluation): State process of evaluation for teachers, as described in the No Child Left Behind (NCLB) legislation. According to NCLB, all teachers are supposed to be highly qualified. New teachers must show their subject knowledge either by passing a test or by holding a degree in the subjects they teach, whereas experienced teachers have the option of meeting a HOUSSE standard, as established by each state. In most states, teachers' years of experience and participation in workshops contribute toward a passing score on these state standards. See also **highly qualified teachers (HQTs)**.

Hutchins, Robert Maynard (1899–1977): The boy wonder of the academic world, who became dean of Yale Law School at age 28 and president of the University of Chicago when he was only 30. At the University of Chicago, he reorganized the curriculum to emphasize undergraduate education. With the help of his friend Mortimer Adler, Hutchins became a national advocate for study of the Great Books, a reading list that included the classic works of Western civilization and spanned the centuries from Homer to Freud. In the mid-1930s, Hutchins began to speak out against progressive education, especially its emphasis on social adjustment, and in favor of a deep, rich liberal education that trained the mind. He was highly controversial among progressives but commanded a wide popular following. He also gained renown for his courageous defense of academic freedom and opposition to McCarthyism. See also **Adler, Mortimer J. (1902–2001); Great Books program**.

immersion: A strategy of teaching students to speak, read, and write in a second language by surrounding them with that language through interaction and instruction. Advocates of immersion contend that such programs help students whose native language is not English to speak and read English as quickly as possible. They maintain that the best language instruction—such as that in the U.S. Army's foreign language school in Monterrey, California, and in the Middlebury College Language Program—relies on immersion techniques. Critics of immersion programs prefer bilingual education on the grounds that immersion is a "sink or swim" approach and does not respect the student's heritage language. See also **acquisition-learning hypothesis; dual immersion**.

Impact Aid: A federal program that provides funds to districts containing students whose families live or work on federal property, such as military bases or American Indian reservations. Funded through Title VIII of the No Child Left Behind Act, this program is also called Public Law 81-874.

incentives for students: Rewards for good academic performance or behavior in school. Grades are the most common incentives for students. In addition, some schools recognize outstanding student achievement at end-of-term events and graduation ceremonies. There are seldom incentives for good behavior, other than the approval of teachers; there are, however, considerable disincentives (punishments) for bad behavior. See also **discipline policy**.

incentives for teachers: A hotly debated reward system for teachers. Some advocate merit pay to recognize teachers whose students get higher test scores than other students with similar characteristics. Teachers' unions oppose this policy on the grounds that the rewards would be unavailable to many people who work in schools, such as art teachers and school secretaries, and that they would cause unnecessary friction among teachers. Some districts have created incentive plans that reward teachers with higher pay if their students achieve more, if they teach in hard-to-staff schools, if they teach subjects in which there is a teacher shortage, if they act as mentors to new teachers, or if they assume additional responsibilities beyond the usual duties of the classroom teacher. See also **bonus pay; merit pay; performance incentive**.

inclusion: The practice of placing students with disabilities in regular classrooms in accordance with federal law. To the maximum extent possible, students with disabilities are supposed to be educated alongside their peers in regular education classrooms unless "the nature or severity of the disability of a child is such that education in regular classes with the use of supplementary aids and services cannot be achieved satisfactorily" (P.L. 94-142 20 U.S.C. 1412(5)(A)). See also **free appropriate public education (FAPE); Individuals with Disabilities Education Act (IDEA); least restrictive environment (LRE); mainstreaming**.

independent reading: Reading that students do on their own, not assigned or chosen by the teacher.

independent schools: Private schools that are not affiliated with any religious organization or public agency. Such schools charge tuition and are usually (but not always, depending on state laws) free from state regulations with regard to curriculum, teacher qualifications, and testing.

independent study: An assignment or a program of study carried out by an individual student outside any regular course and usually supervised by a teacher.

Individualized Education Program (IEP): A highly detailed education plan created for students with learning disabilities by their teachers, parents or guardians, school administrators, school counselors, education psychologists, and other appropriate parties. The plan is tailored to the student's specific needs and abilities and outlines goals for the student to reach. The IEP is a legally binding document that specifies all the accommodations needed for the student to succeed in class and, in particular, to participate in assessments such as standardized tests. See also **free appropriate public education (FAPE); full inclusion program (FIP); Individuals with Disabilities Education Act (IDEA).**

Individualized Transition Program (ITP): A two- to four-year written plan that describes the goals for a student in special education and the steps needed to meet these goals, be they related to academic or to job skills.

Individuals with Disabilities Education Act (IDEA): A law that guarantees children with exceptional needs a free appropriate public education and requires that each student's education be determined on an individual basis and designed to meet his or her unique needs in the least restrictive environment possible. Originally enacted by the U.S. Congress in 1975, IDEA also establishes procedural rights for parents and children. See also **free appropriate public education (FAPE); full inclusion program (FIP); inclusion; Individualized Education Program (IEP); least restrictive environment (LRE).**

inference: The process of drawing a conclusion on the basis of inductive or deductive reasoning.

in-house suspension: The isolation of a student in a special class to punish him or her for a minor offense against classroom, school, or district policies. See also **in-school suspension (ISS).**

inner-city school: An urban, generally public school in a high-poverty area.

innovation: A novel idea, method, or program. U.S. education is infamous for its love of innovation. In fact, many ideas, methods, and programs that are assumed to be innovations are actually revivals of ideas, methods, and programs that were tried 50 or 100 years earlier.

inquiry learning: A process in which students investigate a problem, devise a strategy for solving it, and then actively work toward the solution. See also **discovery learning**.

in-school suspension (ISS): A school policy to provide a program for disruptive students within the school instead of sending them home, where they may be unsupervised and get into more trouble. In-school suspension aims to remove students from the classroom where they misbehaved and put them into a designated program where they can continue to receive instruction under the supervision of a trained teacher. See also **in-house suspension**.

inservice teacher education: Professional development or training for teachers conducted during scheduled work hours. Such classes are intended to sharpen the professional knowledge and skills of teachers who are currently working in the schools, as opposed to preservice education, which is intended for those who have not yet started working as teachers. See also **preservice teacher education**.

inside-out reforms: Reforms that are initiated within a school or school community, involving collaboration among parents, teachers, and students. Contrast **outside-in reforms**.

instantiation: An instance of something; a concrete example of an abstract principle or idea.

instructionally supportive standards-based test: A test whose results provide information on which standards were well taught and which were not.

instructivism: The belief that students learn best when their teachers teach them what they need to know through direct, systematic instruction. Contrast **constructivism**.

integrated language arts: The teaching of grammar, spelling, vocabulary, and writing in the context of literature. Advocates believe that literature gives students opportunities for practical application of these skills in an engaging context. Critics fear that skills are taught only as needed, if at all.

integrated learning: A type of program based on the idea that most learning is interdisciplinary and that people learn best in natural settings rather than in classrooms with a set curriculum and textbooks. Critics contend that this approach is haphazard and fails to teach students the skills and knowledge they need for higher education or the modern workplace. They further charge that making all learning specific to given situations hobbles students' ability to make generalizations, a skill that serves them in unpredictable situations. The term *integrated learning* may also refer to teachers' efforts to combine different subjects, such as social studies and reading, or science and mathematics, in the same lesson.

intellectual capital: The knowledge and skills that a person has acquired through study and practice. Intellectual capital is like money in the bank; the more one has, the more one can accrue in the future because knowledge builds on knowledge.

intelligence quotient (IQ): A measure of general intellectual abilities, as determined by intelligence tests. A child's IQ is the ratio of his or her mental age (as determined through an assessment of verbal, mathematical, and reasoning skills) divided by his or her chronological age, multiplied by 100. The earliest versions of intelligence tests were created in the 1880s by British scientist Francis Galton and were further developed in the early 20th century by French psychologist Alfred Binet. U.S. enthusiasts of IQ testing, like Lewis Terman of Stanford University, believed that intelligence was innate, fixed, and inherited. IQ testing became widespread during and after World War I. Since the 1960s, however, IQ tests have been controversial. Critics claim that they measure only a limited number of intellectual abilities, primarily "school smarts," and that they are biased against members of some minority groups. See also **Terman, Lewis (1877–1956)**.

intelligent design: A concept holding that the origin of the universe was the work of an intelligent designer, not the result of natural selection, as posited in the theory of evolution. Proponents of intelligent design believe that it should be taught alongside evolution as a scientific explanation for the beginning of the universe. The overwhelming majority of scientists and scientific organizations reject intelligent design as junk science that relies on supernatural explanations for scientific phenomena. Efforts by school districts or states to require the teaching of intelligent design have been blocked by federal courts, which have ruled that intelligent design is basically religious in nature, like creationism, and violates the First Amendment prohibition against religious teaching in the public schools. See also **creationism; evolution debate**.

interactive writing: A writing technique in which the student writer works with another party—a teacher or facilitator, one or more classmates, or a computer program—to produce a piece of writing. The writing process generally proceeds according to some predetermined sequence of actions in which parts of the writing are provided by the prompter and other parts are provided, in response, by the student. So, for example, the teacher might generate the first line of a couplet, prompting the student to generate the next one. Proponents of interactive writing say that it can be used to teach students about standard elements of narrative writing, poetry, drama, and nonfiction. Critics say that interactive writing disregards the fact that writing is usually a solitary process.

interclass visitations: Visits by teachers to the classrooms of other teachers to observe their instruction and thereby improve their own practice.

interdisciplinary method: A teaching approach in which teachers of core academic subjects collaborate to plan instruction on a particular subject or theme. For example, students learning about a particular era in history class may study a novel set in that historic period in English class.

interim assessments: Tests that are designed to measure progress during a course of instruction, usually administered partway through the course. Teachers are supposed to use the results of interim assessments to identify students who require extra help and to tailor instruction to the students' needs.

International Baccalaureate (IB): A rigorous international program of study that originated in Switzerland and has spread to more than 100 nations. The program has an explicit syllabus, known to the teachers and students, which is the basis for IB examinations. To be eligible to sit for an IB exam, students must be enrolled in a school that has been accredited through the IB accreditation process and must take the IB course that is the basis for the exam. Students can earn college credit from many universities for IB courses if their exam scores are high enough.

internship: A temporary position in which an individual learns to perform a job or an activity by working under the supervision of an experienced person in the field.

interschool mobility: Transfer of students from one school to another. Such a transfer may be the voluntary decision of students and their families, or it may be arranged by a school system to remove disciplinary problems from a particular school or to exclude low-scoring students from the test population as a way to improve test scores at certain schools.

intersession: School vacation.

intertextual comparison: The interpretive comparison of two or more pieces of writing, such as poems or stories. Students may be asked to make such a comparison during regular instruction or on a reading test.

intervention: A program that does something different from what was done before in an attempt to improve a situation. For example, one intervention may aim to remediate reading failure with a new approach, and another may be designed to help students with special needs. The term is flexible and can apply to a number of situations and programs.

intervention strategies: Programs that provide extra support and resources to help improve student or school performance.

intrinsic motivation: The desire to achieve one's goals, regardless of external rewards, such as grades, honors, or money. Contrast **extrinsic motivation**.

invented spelling: A unique spelling of a word created by a child who has not yet learned the correct spelling. Proponents of invented spelling believe that it encourages students to express their ideas in writing before they have learned to spell. Critics worry that it introduces poor habits early in the learning process. Invented spelling is also referred to as *temporary spelling*, on the assumption that at some point students will learn how to spell the words accurately.

item: A question on a standardized test.

item format: The type of a question on a standardized test—objective, constructed-response, open-response, independent-response, extended-response, and so on.

jigsaw strategy: A cooperative learning technique in which each student within a small work group specializes in one part of a learning unit. Each member of this "home group" is assigned a different aspect of the topic and then meets with members from other groups who are assigned the same material. These "expert groups" discuss and master the material together, after which the experts return to their home groups to teach their portion of the materials to the rest of the group and, in turn, learn from their group partners. Just as in a jigsaw puzzle, each piece is essential for the group's completion of the final product.

jot charting: A pedagogical strategy for teaching reading comprehension. A jot chart is an outline that students develop as they read a passage, to help them identify ideas and facts as they read. Readers who are already fluent may find this technique distracting.

Jukes and Kallikaks: Pseudonyms for two families that were used as examples by early social scientists to warn that criminality and mental retardation were passed along from generation to generation. The Jukes family was portrayed in *The Jukes: A Study in Crime, Pauperism, Disease and Heredity* by Richard L. Dugdale in 1877, and the Kallikaks were the subject of Henry H. Goddard's *The Kallikak Family: A Study in the Heredity of Feeble-Mindedness* (1912). The names of these two families entered into common parlance as exemplars of what happens when people with bad genes breed and proliferate.

Jumpstart: A program to promote the social development and literacy of preschool children by pairing them with trained college students in a one-to-one relationship. Jumpstart was founded at Yale University in 1993 to improve early childhood services and to offer college students an opportunity for public service.

K–8 school: A school that begins with kindergarten and ends with 8th grade, combining elementary and middle schools.

K–12: The customary spectrum of grades in a school system, beginning with kindergarten and ending with the senior year in high school. A K–12 system is typically composed of elementary schools, middle schools, and high schools.

K–14: Kindergarten through community college.

K–16: Kindergarten through the end of a four-year college.

Kilpatrick, William Heard (1871–1965): One of the most influential figures in the progressive education movement. A disciple of John Dewey, Kilpatrick aspired to be the chief exponent of Dewey's ideas. At Teachers College, Columbia University, he taught tens of thousands of future teachers and administrators. Kilpatrick was a champion of child-centered education and opposed a set curriculum planned in advance of instruction. In 1918, he devised the *project method*, an approach aiming to make learning more relevant and meaningful by encouraging students to create their own projects according to their interests instead of studying subject matter. See also **project-based learning**.

---

kindergarten: Literally a "children's garden" in German; a class where young children, around age 5, prepare for 1st grade. Kindergarten is a place where children learn basic social skills through play, exercise, handicrafts, and the arts. As preschool programs proliferate, kindergarten has increasingly become a class that also teaches the uses of letters and numbers. The first kindergarten was founded in 1840 in Germany by Friedrich Froebel. The first public kindergarten in the United States was established in 1873 by education reformer Susan Blow in St. Louis, Missouri. See also **Froebel, Friedrich (1782–1852)**.

Knowledge Is Power Program (KIPP): A network of middle schools and high schools, founded by David Levin and Michael Feinberg, located in inner-city neighborhoods. Some KIPP schools are charter schools, and others are regular public schools; all have an extended school day. KIPP schools accept students regardless of prior academic performance, conduct, or socioeconomic status and aim to inspire their students to have a positive attitude, work hard, and aspire to go to college.

Kumon method: A private tutoring program that teaches mathematics and reading. Developed in Japan, the Kumon method is a form of mastery learning, based on the idea that students should thoroughly understand each step in the learning process before moving on to the next one.

K-W-L chart: A graphic organizer for reading and gathering information that activates students' prior knowledge of a topic and helps them take inventory of what they want to learn about it. *K* stands for What I *Know*; *W* stands for What I *Want* to Know; and *L* stands for What I *Learned*.

Lake Wobegon effect: The tendency to overestimate one's achievements and abilities in relation to others; in education specifically, the tendency of states and districts to inflate their test scores by various artful means to please the public. This term was first applied to education in 1988 by psychiatrist John J. Cannell in his report *Nationally Normed Elementary Achievement Testing in America's Public Schools: How All 50 States Are Above the National Average.* The report found that student performance in nearly every U.S. state was reportedly above the national average. This "effect" was not merely a statistical fluke but evidence that states had purposely set low standards. Dr. Cannell's findings evoked a familiar line, coined by humorist Garrison Keillor, that in the mythical town of Lake Wobegon, "all the women are strong, all the men are good-looking, and all the children are above average."

language arts: See **English language arts (ELA).**

large-scale assessments: Standardized tests that are administered to a large population—for example, all the students within a given state, or a sample of all the students in the United States. The National Assessment of Educational Progress, a federally funded testing program, is a large-scale assessment; it administers tests of different academic subjects to state and national samples of students, which are then adjusted (weighted) to represent the student populations of the different states and of the nation.

latchkey children: Children who go to an empty home at the end of the school day. The "latchkey" is usually worn around the child's neck or hidden under a doormat or other object near the entrance. The phenomenon of latchkey kids is associated with the relatively recent growth in the proportion of working mothers in the United States and has led to demands for after-school programs to keep the children safe and usefully occupied.

Lau v. Nichols: A 1974 decision by the U.S. Supreme Court that became the basis for most federal and state bilingual education programs. In the case, the Court ruled against the San Francisco school system for failing to provide English language instruction to limited-English-proficient students from China. The Court directed the school district to create special language programs for these students but did not prescribe a specific remedy, ruling that the district could teach English to the students, offer them instruction in Chinese, or choose a different approach.

learner-centered classroom: A classroom in which students are expected to choose their own learning goals and activities. The approach assumes that children naturally want to learn and will learn more enthusiastically when they are working on projects of their own selection. Their teachers, at the same time, are expected to be able to gauge and tailor activities to students' different learning styles. Also called *learner-driven classroom*. See also **student-centered education**. Contrast **teacher-centered instruction; teacher-directed classroom**.

learner outcomes: Specific expectations of what students are supposed to know or be able to do as a result of a specific course or learning activity.

learning: The process of gaining knowledge, skills, or understanding through study, instruction, or experience.

learning disability (LD): A physical, cognitive, neurological, or psychological disorder that impedes a student's ability to learn, such as dyslexia. LD is sometimes used as a nonspecific catchall label for students who are not progressing in school at their peers' pace. Such students may need better instruction rather than assignment to special education classes.

learning how to learn: What may be the most important goal of schooling—teaching students how to become lifelong learners. Some people believe that knowledge becomes obsolete so quickly that "mere" facts are unimportant in comparison with learning how to learn. It is unwise to set up a false dichotomy between knowledge and learning how to learn, however, because the two are integrally connected. Youngsters need to know how to learn, *and* they need a fund of background knowledge. If they lack either the tools for self-education or the knowledge that is the foundation of learning, then they cannot become lifelong learners.

learning lab: A room in a school that has been set aside for academic support activities for students. See also **resource room**.

learning progressions: Detailed descriptions of the order in which students should learn about various topics, from grade to grade, based on what they understand when they begin school and what they are supposed to know at different points in their education. The term also refers to a logical, coherent sequence of lessons, each building on the previous one, with the goal of developing student comprehension of important concepts in different content areas.

learning style: The mode of learning that is most effective for a given student. Advocates of learning style theory claim that people learn through various channels—visual, tactile, auditory, written, or kinesthetic, for example—and that one or more of these will be the dominant learning style for a particular student. Some educators claim that boys and girls have different learning styles, or that different racial and ethnic groups have distinctive learning styles. Learning style theory calls for teachers both to figure out the distinct learning style of each student and to tailor their instruction accordingly—a task that critics claim is nearly impossible. At best, it's a heavy burden: according to learning style theory, a student's low achievement could be attributed not to a lack of effort on the student's part but to the teacher's failure to identify and address the student's unique learning style. See also **modality**.

learning trajectory: The "arc" or aggregate of a student's learning, resulting from careful curricular design that identifies the kind of instruction, activities, technological tools, and other resources that are necessary to foster learning.

learning walk: A structured process in which an administrator "walks" through classrooms to observe, ask questions, and interact with teachers and students to make sure that everyone is focused on learning. The learning walk, a term coined by Lauren Resnick of the University of Pittsburgh, is supposed to incorporate three principles: academic rigor, clear expectations, and accountable talk. The administrator uses this technique to demonstrate instructional leadership or to impose and enforce a uniform approach to teaching.

least restrictive environment (LRE): A term with legal force that is part of the Individuals with Disabilities Education Act. *LRE* refers to a setting where students with disabilities can be educated alongside their peers without disabilities to the maximum extent possible. The law states that students with disabilities should be taught in regular education classes unless their disabilities are so severe as to make mainstreaming inappropriate for them. See also **inclusion; Individuals with Disabilities Education Act (IDEA)**.

lecture: Instruction given by a teacher to impart information directly to a class. For many years, lecture was considered an efficient means of summarizing information and presenting issues to students, and it continues to be the dominant mode of instruction in colleges and universities. It's a different story in the K–12 world, however: although some teachers, especially at the high school level, still deliver lectures, this method is now infrequently encountered in elementary and middle schools. In their pedagogical training, U.S. educators are taught to avoid the lecture style of instruction in favor of individualized instruction, cooperative learning, small group activities, project-based learning, and other indirect methods of teaching.

left-brain/right-brain theory: The theory that each hemisphere in the brain specializes in different ways of thinking and that schools should adjust instruction accordingly. The left side of the brain is said to be logical, sequential, rational, and analytical, and to examine problems by breaking them into parts, whereas the right side of the brain is said to be random, intuitive, holistic, and subjective, and to look at problems as wholes. The theory suggests that traditional schooling favors left-brain thinkers while disadvantaging right-brain thinkers, who are aesthetic, creative, spontaneous, and imaginative. However, cognitive scientists say that brain research is insufficient to carry the weight of this theory and in general does not yet provide clear direction to teachers about classroom instruction. See also **brain-based education**.

leveled library: A collection of books or other reading materials in balanced literacy classrooms and schools that are organized by their levels of difficulty, beginning with easy books for beginners and ranging to relatively complex books for advanced readers. For each grade, there might be three or four (or more) different levels of books. As students advance to increasingly more difficult books, the teacher continually assesses their progress. Leveled libraries are generally placed in a central area, like the school library, or in individual classrooms. See also **shared book room**.

leveled readers: Books that have been designed or selected according to how well they match students' reading ability, usually found in balanced literacy schools.

liberal education: Education that places a high value on learning for its own sake rather than for vocational or utilitarian ends. A liberal education usually includes the study of history, literature, the sciences, mathematics, the arts, and a foreign language. The study of these subjects provides insight into the most important realms of knowledge about human society as well as access to the tools, devised over many generations, for understanding the natural world. Knowledge of this kind opens the doors to higher education and is considered necessary to become an educated person and to think clearly, with a free, informed, and unbiased mind.

library: A space in the school that contains books of all kinds, both fiction and nonfiction; magazines; maps; computer terminals; videos; and other media intended to communicate ideas and knowledge. A library is not to be confused with a shared book room: it contains many more books, and they are not leveled by grade. In addition, students are free to read library books that are above or below their presumed reading level. Traditionally, the school library has a trained librarian who assists students in locating what they need.

life adjustment movement: A movement in the 1940s and 1950s to reduce the academic demands of schooling and instead infuse it with activities connected to everyday life, thus "adjusting" students to their likely futures. This movement received enthusiastic support from the federal Office of Education and state education departments and had a broad influence on schools at that time. The movement called for the provision of academic programs for 20 percent of students, vocational education for another 20 percent, and "life adjustment education" for the remaining 60 percent of students, who allegedly lacked the motivation or intellect for either academic or vocational studies.

lifelong learning: The continuation of learning throughout one's lifetime. No single instructional pattern is guaranteed to inspire students to remain intellectually alive, but all sorts of schools have produced lifelong learners: public schools, Catholic schools, independent schools, traditional schools, progressive schools. There is no magic formula that ignites this wonderful desire to learn and continue learning as one ages.

limited-English-proficient (LEP): Label applied to a student from a non-English-speaking background who has not yet learned English. *LEP student* is often used interchangeably with the term *English language learner*. See also **English language learner (ELL)**. Contrast **fluent-English-proficient (FEP)**.

literacy block: A period of time set aside in the elementary school day for reading and language activities, usually as part of a balanced literacy program. A typical literacy block would include small-group and individual activities; examples of such activities include minilessons, read-alouds, shared reading, guided reading, independent reading, guided writing, modeled writing, independent writing, shared writing, interactive writing, and student conferences. Part of the literacy block is set aside for word work, during which students learn about phonics, vocabulary, and phonemic awareness.

literacy center: A place in the classroom where students gather in small groups to read on their own.

literacy circle: A group of students who are reading or learning to read and who are encouraged by the teacher to discuss what they are reading or learning.

literacy-focused time: Class time devoted to reading and learning to read.

literacy stages: The developmental stages of learning to read. Students begin as nonreaders and progress through specific stages to become proficient readers. Literacy educators do not agree on the names of these stages or on how many stages there are, although a common progression includes the preprint stage, the emergent literacy stage, the early literacy stage, and the independent literacy stage.

literate: In education, a descriptor of students who can read and write at the level expected for their age and grade; in general, a descriptor of an educated person, able to read and write and possessing an extensive vocabulary and a rich fund of knowledge about important aspects of society and the world.

literature circle: A small, temporary discussion group of students who have chosen to read the same work of literature. Literature circles are intended to engage students by putting them in charge of their own learning: the students, not the teacher, decide which book the circle will read, and each student in the circle has a specific role during discussion sessions. For example, one student may be in charge of writing down questions to discuss, another of identifying important passages in the work, another of finding connections between the work discussed and something else that the group knows about, and another of discussing unusual words in the text. Literature circles meet regularly during class time, and the discussion roles change at each meeting. When the circle completes a book, its members discuss their literary work with the rest of the class. Literature circles introduce two new elements to English class: first, teachers relinquish their role as the adult who is responsible for selecting important literature that students should read; and second, the circles replace the traditional practice of having an entire English class read and discuss the same work of literature under the guidance of the teacher.

Local Education Agency (LEA): A public board of education, or other public authority within a state, that maintains administrative control of public elementary or secondary schools in a city, county, township, school district, or other political subdivision of a state.

longitudinal data: Data (e.g., achievement data for a specific group of students) that are tracked over time. In education, the ability to track students as they progress through the school system is important for evaluating the possible contribution that schools, specific programs, and teachers make to student performance, and for accurately tracking the progress of specific subgroups of students.

look-say method: A now-obsolete way to teach reading in which beginning readers memorize common whole words presented in texts that use these words repeatedly. The famous Dick and Jane readers were the prime example of look-say reading books. Although the look-say method was commonplace in most reading textbooks in the 1940s and 1950s, it was discredited when Rudolf Flesch published his best-selling attack *Why Johnny Can't Read*. See also **whole-word method**.

looping: The practice of having one teacher educate the same group of students for more than one school year, rather than assigning students to different teachers and classes every year. According to advocates, looping increases instructional time for students; builds strong bonds between teachers and students and among students themselves; and increases teachers' sense of responsibility for their students. Critics say that students may suffer if they have a weak teacher for multiple years and that they lose the opportunity to encounter a wide range of friends and teachers.

loose coupling: A description of the relationship between institutions that operate relatively autonomously but share similar purposes—for example, schools and colleges. Sometimes even elementary schools, middle schools, and high schools are said to be loosely coupled because of the discontinuities among them. See also **articulation**.

lower-order critical thinking: Simple recall of memorized facts without comprehension of their meaning or context.

low-performing schools: Schools whose students consistently earn lower-than-average test scores, as compared with schools with similar demographics, and make little or no progress toward improving their academic performance over a number of years. See also **failing schools**. Contrast **high-performing schools**.

low-stakes test: A test that has few consequences for students—for example, a test whose results are used to rate or rank schools but not to assign specific rewards or sanctions to students on the basis of their performance. Students who take a low-stakes test may receive their scores, but the scores do not affect their grades, college admission, or anything else that is important to them. See also **no-stakes test**. Contrast **high-stakes test**.

magnet school: A school that emphasizes a particular discipline, such as science, mathematics, the arts, or technology, and aims to recruit students from different parts of the school district. Magnet schools were first created to reduce racial segregation by encouraging students to transfer voluntarily to a new school outside their neighborhood instead of being compelled to transfer by district officials or by court order.

mainstreaming: The practice of placing students with disabilities in regular education classes. To most people, mainstreaming is synonymous with *inclusion*. Some, however, see these as two different practices, with mainstreaming defined as the inclusion of students with disabilities in nonacademic activities and inclusion defined as teaching all subjects to all students, with accommodations where necessary. See also **free and appropriate public education (FAPE); inclusion; Individuals with Disabilities Education Act (IDEA).**

mandated costs: School district expenditures that are required by federal or state law, by court decisions, or by voter-initiated measures.

manipulatives: Any physical objects (such as coins, sticks, dice, or blocks) that can be used to represent a mathematics problem or develop a concept. Although customarily used in the elementary grades, some mathematics educators recommend their use even in high school.

Mann, Horace (1796–1859): One of the founders of U.S. public education. Mann was a lawyer and state legislator who became state secretary of education in Massachusetts in 1837. In this role, he agitated on behalf of free, universal public education, well-educated teachers, well-furnished schoolhouses, higher pay for teachers, nonsectarian instruction, and a sound curriculum. Mann argued persuasively for the economic benefits of public education. His prolific writings, especially his annual reports, were widely read (and continue to be); they generated support for education reform, not only in Massachusetts but also throughout the United States.

mapping: The human mind's creation of an abstract model of relationships existing in the external world. For example, every child creates a cognitive map of the kinship system in his or her family or culture.

masking card: A card that teachers use during literacy instruction to hide certain words, parts of words, or phrases to focus students' attention on the text that remains uncovered.

Maslow's hierarchy of needs: A theory developed by U.S. psychologist Abraham Maslow in the latter half of the 20th century that describes human behavior in relation to the basic and higher needs that people experience in their lives. The theory posits that only after individuals' basic needs (physiological needs, safety needs, needs for love and affection, and needs for esteem) are met can they seek to satisfy their higher needs of self-actualization.

master teacher: A teacher who is recognized by fellow educators and by students alike as among the very best in a school. Students seem to know who the master teachers are; they seek out their classes and remember them many years after their student days. Such teachers inspire students to love learning and often influence their life choices. Numerous school districts have created programs to identify master teachers and to reward them for coaching or mentoring other teachers. In addition, many universities and school districts have established programs to train master teachers; however, the effects of such programs are inconclusive because there is no known formula for producing teachers who will reach the pinnacle of their profession.

mastery: A level of achievement at which a student can be said to understand a concept thoroughly or demonstrate a skill flawlessly. An assessment may attempt to define mastery as the ability to consistently achieve scores at some predetermined level (e.g., a score of 85 or above).

mastery learning: An instructional method developed by Benjamin Bloom that presumes that all students can learn if they are provided with the appropriate learning conditions. Under this approach, students learn new lessons one step at a time, advancing to the next level only after they have demonstrated proficiency in the current level's material. See also **continuous progress; Kumon method**.

material-based instruction: A teaching technique that relies on printed materials handed out by the teacher to the students in the class. This is a technical term for a common practice.

Mathematically Correct: An organization founded by a group of parents—including mathematicians and engineers—in California to oppose constructivist mathematics programs, which they referred to as *new new math*, *whole math*, and *fuzzy math*. Mathematically Correct joined with and inspired similar organizations in other states. The organization was very effective in persuading the California State Board of Education to adopt mathematics standards in 1997 that restored the traditional teaching of mathematics in every grade. See also **fuzzy math; math wars; new math; new new math; whole math**.

mathematics: The study of numbers, patterns, shapes, and spatial configurations, as well as their interrelations, measurement, operations that can be performed on them, and generalizations that can be made about them. In U.S. schools, mathematics usually begins with the study of algorithms for addition, subtraction, multiplication, and division, which are referred to as basic skills. In middle school and high school, students learn such subjects as algebra, geometry, probability and statistics, trigonometry, and elementary calculus.

---

math wars: Debates about the proper subjects and methods of mathematics instruction. In the 1960s and 1970s, a math war was fought between proponents and opponents of the new math, which introduced logic and set theory to elementary and secondary mathematics curricula. In the 1990s, a math war broke out between proponents and opponents of discovery approaches to mathematics instruction. On one side were adherents of the standards promulgated in 1989 by the National Council of Teachers of Mathematics (NCTM), which promoted a philosophy of teaching mathematics centered mainly on inquiry and multiple approaches to finding solutions; on the other side were critics who believed that the NCTM standards ignored the teaching of basic skills and lacked content and specificity. See also **fuzzy math; Mathematically Correct; new math; new new math; whole math**.

---

matrix sampling: The division of a set of test items into different versions of an assessment form. With this method, no single student takes the entire test; instead, different portions are given to representative samples of students, and group scores may be calculated for schools, districts, or states (but not for individuals). This design is used by several large-scale testing programs, including the National Assessment of Educational Progress.

Matthew effect: A term referring to a line in the New Testament that reads, "For unto every one that hath shall be given, and he shall have abundance: but from him that hath not shall be taken away even that which he hath" (Matthew 25:29). This is usually taken to mean that the rich get richer and the poor get poorer. In education, the phrase was popularized by psychologist Keith Stanovich, who maintained that students who are early readers continue over time to accumulate advantage over those who have difficulty learning to read, because the former group reads more, accrues a larger vocabulary, and thus ends up learning more.

McGuffey readers: A celebrated series of six reading textbooks created by Rev. William Holmes McGuffey that were used by millions of students in the United States in the latter half of the 19th century and the early 20th century. The books were designed to increase in difficulty, from beginning to advanced reading levels, as students progressed through the series. They were moralistic in tone, intending to provide models of good behavior and civic virtue. The fifth and sixth books contained excellent literature, including excerpts from leading English and American authors, such as William Shakespeare and Nathaniel Hawthorne. Because so many children used the same textbooks, the McGuffey readers created a common lexicon of literary allusions for several generations of Americans.

meaning from print: Understanding what the text says, relying on context and prior knowledge.

mean score: The arithmetic average of a set of scores. It is found by adding all the scores in the distribution and dividing that sum by the total number of scores.

media center: A library that contains technology, such as computers with Internet access and audiovisual equipment and materials.

median: The 50th percentile, or the number that divides the upper half of a sample, population, or distribution from the lower half. The median of a list of test scores, for example, can be found by arranging all the scores in order from lowest to highest value and picking the middle one.

media specialist: A librarian who is trained in the use of new technologies.

meeting the needs of the whole child: A slogan that was popular with the child-centered wing of the progressive education movement in the first half of the 20th century. It meant that schools must consider all the child's needs—not only academic needs but also social, emotional, and physical ones. The progressive movement had a large effect on the practice of schools, prompting them to hire nurses, social workers, and guidance counselors; to provide time for play; to serve nutritious meals; and to screen students for vision and hearing problems. See also **teach the child, not the subject**.

---

memorization: The act of committing information—such as words, facts, numbers, or literary selections—to memory, with the result of being able to recall it at will. Although memorization has long been derided as a mechanical, rote way of learning, it has its uses. For example, memorizing the multiplication tables enables students to quickly and automatically recall the product of two simple numbers without having to think about it or locate a calculator. It is also deeply satisfying to memorize beautiful poems and know them by heart, so that they may be recited aloud to a group or recalled in the quiet of the night simply for one's own pleasure. Moreover, children generally do not dislike the task of memorization and in fact often take great pride in memorizing baseball statistics, the names of dinosaurs, the lyrics of songs, and various obscure marginalia. See also **rote learning**.

---

mentee: One who receives guidance or coaching from a more experienced person.

---

mentor: A trusted counselor or guide who tutors or coaches a newcomer or novice.

---

meritocracy: A system that rewards achievement rather than inherited privilege. Public schooling and standardized tests are widely considered essential elements of the American meritocracy. Critics of meritocracy complain that it produces unequal outcomes. Supporters of meritocracy reply that any way of distributing life's rewards that does not recognize talent and effort would promote mediocrity and lead to a dull, bland society.

---

merit pay: An adjustment in teacher compensation to confer additional financial rewards on highly effective teachers, normally determined by the academic achievement of their students. So, for example, a teacher whose students make larger-than-expected gains on local or state tests would receive higher pay than a teacher whose students did poorly on the same tests. Also called *performance pay*. See also **bonus pay; incentives for teachers; performance incentive**.

meta-analysis: The statistical analysis of the results of multiple studies, which generally yields a more reliable estimate of an effect than does a single study. A summary review of hundreds of studies of the effects of homework, for example, is far more valuable than examining only one or two such studies.

metacognition: An awareness of one's own thinking processes; the process of regulating one's own learning by reviewing one's knowledge and methods of problem solving.

metacognitive objectives: Instructional objectives intended to demonstrate that students are aware of how they learn, that they reflect on how they know what they know, and that they have the ability to think about their own processes of thinking.

METCO: A Massachusetts program to transfer African American students from Boston and Springfield to suburban schools, both to improve racial balance in the schools and to provide a higher-quality education to those who choose to participate in the program. Both the students and the suburban districts volunteer to be part of METCO.

Mickey Mouse courses: A term used by teachers to describe required courses in pedagogy that have neither intellectual substance nor practical value in the classroom.

micromanagement: A style of leadership in which the person at the top is extremely prescriptive and tries to control the actions (and sometimes the thoughts) of those below him or her.

Middle College High School: A high school located on a college campus that provides at-risk and underserved students with a good-quality high school education and the chance to earn college credits. The faculties of the high school and the college work closely together and share resources and facilities. The high school emphasizes small classes and close interactions between students and adults. Students, who begin in 9th grade, do not usually earn an associate's degree. See also **Early College High School.**

---

middle school: The school that follows elementary school and precedes high school. It is sometimes referred to as an *intermediate school* and was previously called *junior high school*. Middle schools' grade configurations vary; common ones include grades 4–8, 6–8, and 7–9. Some districts, in response to poor discipline and low achievement, have reverted to a K–8 pattern, effectively eliminating the middle school altogether.

---

migrant education: Academic and supportive services for students who are children of families that migrate to find work. Special federal funds are allocated for such schooling from the Office of Migrant Education in the U.S. Department of Education.

---

minilesson: A short period of instruction (approximately 10–15 minutes long) that is an integral part of the constructivist workshop model in a balanced literacy program. The steps of a minilesson include (1) *connection*, during which the teacher connects the lesson's content to what has come before, including students' own experience, and names the strategy being taught (the *teaching point*); (2) *teaching*, during which the teacher states explicitly and then models what students are supposed to learn; (3) *active involvement*, during which students engage with the content or try out the strategy; and (4) *link*, during which the teacher restates the teaching point and tells students to add it to their repertoire. Following this minilesson is an independent work period during which the teacher walks around and comments on the work of individual students. After about 30 minutes comes the *share* stage, when the teacher draws attention to the good work of a student and again highlights the minilesson's teaching point. These steps are part of the *architecture of minilessons* developed by Lucy Calkins of Teachers College, Columbia University, as the workshop model. See also **workshop model**.

---

minischool: A small high school, sometimes with a theme, such as arts, technology, or a specific career. Minischools are usually created by dividing up existing large high schools into three or more small schools within the same building. See also **school within a school (SWAS); small learning community (SLC)**.

misarticulation: A type of speech problem that prevents a student from being able to produce sounds correctly, often characterized by the substitution, omission, distortion, or addition of phonemes.

miscue: A term originally used in billiards to describe an error that occurs when the cue stick just misses the ball. In education, reading researcher Kenneth Goodman coined the term to describe any departure from the text during oral reading. Educators— mostly whole-language adherents—use the word *miscue* instead of *error* to suggest that mistakes are not random but occur because the reader is using specific but inappropriate strategies to make sense of text. From this standpoint, not all errors (or miscues) are equal; some represent more highly developed reading skills than others. In addition, *miscue analysis* is used to diagnose the reader's understanding of the text, determining which strategies the reader is using or lacking and what kinds of additional instruction might be helpful. In Goodman's model, reading is an active process in which readers use their language and experience to seek meaning.

modality: A means by which learning occurs, as, for example, through visual or kinesthetic experience. Some education theorists maintain that each student has his or her own learning style. Critics contend that it would be very difficult to teach a class of 25 or more students if each one has a distinctive learning style. See also **learning style**.

mode: In statistics, the score or value that occurs most frequently in a probability distribution.

module: A unit that covers a single topic in a course of study.

Montessori method: A philosophy of education for young children developed in Italy by Dr. Maria Montessori, similar to U.S. child-centered progressivism but far more strictly designed, structured, and orderly than the typical U.S. progressive school. Trained as an engineer and a physician, Montessori opened her Casa dei Bambini (House of Children) in 1907 in the slums of Rome to demonstrate her pedagogical ideas. In a Montessori school, children are surrounded by carefully selected materials and are given many opportunities to pursue projects on their own.

motivation: The will to accomplish a task or reach a goal. Educators are perennially in search of a technique or philosophy that will motivate students to study and learn. If found, this strategy would constitute the Holy Grail of education, or the royal road to learning. Until the middle of the 20th century, students were motivated to learn by their desire to win the praise of adults, to earn a diploma, or to gain admission to college. Almost every reform proposed in the last century—from small schools to vocational education to project-based learning to graduation tests—has been intended to improve student learning by stimulating their motivation.

multicultural education: An approach to education that draws on the historical, cultural, and scientific contributions and experiences of a wide variety of racial, ethnic, national, and cultural groups.

multigrade classroom: A classroom where students of different ages and grades are taught together, often in such configurations as grades 1–3 or grades 3–5, although any combination of contiguous grades is possible. Such classrooms have their roots in the many one-room schoolhouses that used to exist in the United States, where children of all ages learned in the same classroom. As enrollments grew, the one-room schoolhouse was replaced by graded schools. It is only fairly recently that the multigrade classroom—also called the *ungraded classroom*—has returned in some schools.

multimedia learning: Educational programs that integrate different content forms, such as text, images, video, audio, and computer applications, to communicate ideas and information.

multiple-choice item: A test question accompanied by a list of response options that include the correct answer and several incorrect alternatives. The student chooses one of the response options by checking a box or filling in a bubble. See also **distracter; foils; stem**.

---

multiple intelligences (MI): The theory that people have many ways of demonstrating their capabilities and that rather than being a single entity, intelligence is made up of distinct learning proficiencies that can work individually or together. In 1983, psychologist Howard Gardner introduced the concept of multiple intelligences in his book *Frames of Mind* to show that the usual school-based emphasis on rationality and logic is not the only way to be "intelligent." There is now a huge following for MI; many schools have adopted some version of it, and related training and professional development programs have proliferated. Gardner originally identified seven intelligences, only the first two of which are typically valued by schools: verbal-linguistic (the ability to use language to convey information well and to analyze language use); logical-mathematical (the capacity to analyze problems logically, grasp abstractions, recognize codes and patterns, carry out mathematical operations, and investigate issues scientifically); visual-spatial (the ability to recognize and manipulate the relationships of objects, concepts, or images in different fields or dimensions); musical-rhythmic (sensitivity to pitch and rhythm of sounds, as well as skill in performance, composition, and appreciation of musical patterns); bodily-kinesthetic (the ability to use body movement to connect with information, solve problems, and convey ideas); interpersonal (the awareness of others' intentions, motivations, and feelings, and the ability to interact with others with understanding); and intrapersonal (the capacity to understand oneself and to recognize and appreciate one's own feelings, fears, and motivations). Gardner subsequently added an eighth intelligence: naturalist intelligence, or the ability to recognize, categorize, and draw on certain features of the natural environment. Critics say that these intelligences are actually aptitudes or abilities, or variations of rational thinking, rather than what most people consider general intelligence, and that no one can function successfully in the modern world without the linguistic and logical skills valued by schools.

---

multiple learning modalities: Different ways of gaining information, knowledge, and skills, such as seeing, listening, moving, touching, reading, engaging in hands-on experiments, conducting research, performing reenactments, role playing, and so on.

---

multiple literacies: A term denoting the belief that the traditional definition of literacy as the ability to read and write is inadequate or even obsolete in today's world. According to some, *multiple literacies* refers to the ability to understand and navigate electronic media, such as computers, handheld organizers, cell phones, and the Internet. Others hold that the term refers to the ability to construct, deconstruct, and reconstruct popular culture. In addition, the principle of multiple literacies has political connotations, with advocates of critical theory maintaining that the traditional European American view of literacy must expand to acknowledge the voices of people in other cultures who up to now have been marginalized and ignored by postcolonial airs of superiority.

---

multiple perspectives: The representation of more than one point of view in describing historical events. The assumption behind the concept of multiple perspectives is that only the powerful and the victorious get to write history; accordingly, advocates of multiple perspectives believe that other voices, especially those of racial and ethnic minorities and women, should be included in historical narratives. Textbooks try to achieve this goal, but in practice it is daunting to tell a story from multiple points of view without confusing readers.

---

multiplication tables: A grid containing sequential numbers on each of two axes and the products of those numbers in the individual cells of the grid. The multiplication tables simplify the process of adding an integer to itself a specified number of times (e.g., $6 \times 6 = 36$) or extending the process to other numbers (e.g., $6 \times 4 = 24$). The multiplication tables may be memorized by rote or analyzed to comprehend why they work. However they are learned, knowing them by heart is a boon to students and adults alike in solving mathematical problems and performing calculations that arise in everyday life.

name and shame: A derogatory term for a reform strategy that involves *naming* schools or people whose performance is poor, thus presumably *shaming* them into trying harder, improving, or seeking help from others.

narrative evaluation: A qualitative assessment of an individual's performance consisting of written anecdotal feedback.

National Assessment Governing Board (NAGB): The bipartisan, independent board of citizens that supervises the federal National Assessment of Educational Progress (NAEP). The members of the NAGB are appointed by the U.S. secretary of education and include governors, state legislators, state superintendents of education, teachers, principals, members of the business community, and members of the public. The board's role is to safeguard the quality, the political independence, and the professional integrity of the NAEP.

National Assessment of Educational Progress (NAEP): A national testing program that is funded by the U.S. Department of Education and supervised by the National Assessment Governing

Board. NAEP assesses what U.S. students know and can do in various subject areas, including reading, writing, mathematics, science, history, geography, the arts, and other fields. NAEP tests are administered to random samples of students in grades 4, 8, and 12 in certain subjects at periodic intervals. NAEP tests have been given to national samples since 1969, and state testing began in 1992. Since 2003, every state has been required to administer NAEP tests of reading and mathematics every other year as part of the federal No Child Left Behind legislation. NAEP is known as the Nation's Report Card and is considered the gold standard of educational testing.

National Association of Independent Schools (NAIS): A membership organization that represents nearly 1,200 independent day schools, boarding schools, and combination day and boarding schools. These include a range of schools: elementary and secondary; coeducational and single-sex; and urban, suburban, and rural.

National Board certification: A certificate awarded by the National Board for Professional Teaching Standards (NBPTS) attesting that a teacher meets the National Board standards for professional teaching excellence. NBPTS was established in 1987 following the recommendations of a report called *A Nation Prepared: Teachers for the 21st Century* by the Carnegie Forum on Education and the Economy's Task Force on Teaching as a Profession. The purpose of the certification process is to make teaching more professional, to recognize outstanding teachers, and to create a credential that will be accepted by different districts and states. To earn a certificate, the candidate must complete a two-part assessment. First, the teacher submits a portfolio that provides evidence of good teaching, such as videotapes of classroom teaching, lesson plans, student work samples, and self-evaluative essays. Next, the teacher participates in a daylong evaluation of his or her knowledge of curriculum design, good teaching practice, assessment of student learning, and subject matter.

National Education Association (NEA): The larger of the United States' two major teachers unions, the other being the American Federation of Teachers (AFT). Like the AFT, the NEA represents teachers and other school personnel. Its total membership is over 3 million. Founded in the mid–19th century, the NEA was for many decades dominated by school superintendents and leaders of higher education. In the 1960s, it became a union of professionals. In 1998, the NEA and the AFT attempted to merge, but the effort was rejected by members of the AFT. However, locals of the two unions have merged in several states.

National Endowment for the Arts (NEA): A federal agency that provides grants to artists and to state and local organizations to support the arts.

National Endowment for the Humanities (NEH): A federal agency that provides grants to individuals and to state and local organizations to support research, education, preservation, and public programs in the humanities, which include history, philosophy, literature, language, ethics, and archaeology.

nationally normed assessment: A standardized test that has been administered to a national control group reflecting the demographic profile of the target population (e.g., 4th graders) throughout the country. The scores of all subsequent test takers are then compared with the scores of this control (or *norming*) group.

national percentile: A number representing the percentage of students from the nation as a whole who scored at or below a given point. For example, a student who scored at the 90th percentile would have scored higher than 89 percent of the students from the national sample who took that test.

National Reading Panel (NRP): A commission of reading experts assembled by the National Institute of Child Health and Human Development, at the request of the U.S. Congress in 1997, to assess the effectiveness of different approaches to reading instruction. Its 2000 report, called *Teaching Children to Read*, was influential in encouraging textbook publishers to include phonics as an important part of early reading instruction and in influencing the Reading First portion of the No Child Left Behind legislation.

National School Lunch Program (NSLP): A federal program that provides free or reduced-price lunch and/or breakfast to students from low-income families. The proportion of students participating in this meal program is used as a way to measure the poverty level of a school or district population. The number of students in this program can affect schools' or districts' eligibility for funding aimed at helping lower-income families.

national standards: An agreement at the national level about what students are supposed to learn in a given subject area in each grade level. Such standards are usually *content standards* (what is to be learned), but they may also be *performance standards* (the level of proficiency that students should achieve as they advance in their study of the subject). The United States does not have such standards, although textbooks and nationally standardized tests presume their de facto existence.

native language: The primary or first language spoken by an individual.

New American Schools Development Corporation (NASDC): A private, nonprofit organization established in 1991 at the behest of top officials of the U.S. Department of Education in the administration of President George H. W. Bush. Secretary of Education Lamar Alexander and Deputy Secretary of Education David Kearns urged U.S. business and industry leaders to launch NASDC to stimulate innovation by commissioning new designs for schooling. NASDC raised about $50 million, held a design competition, and awarded grants to 11 organizations to create "break-the-mold" schools. These schools were supposed to transform U.S. education by showing what a completely redesigned school could accomplish. As yet, this goal has not been reached. See also **break-the-mold schools**.

new math: An effort in the late 1950s and the 1960s to revolutionize mathematics instruction by teaching the structure of the discipline—especially basic set theory, number theory, and logic—rather than conventional skills. It was not a single program but a collection of concepts that emerged from various groups funded by the federal National Science Foundation. Students and teachers encountered the new math as a collection of concepts like sets, numeration in bases other than 10, and prime numbers. For a time, every textbook series embraced the new math, but teachers complained that it was difficult to teach, mathematicians found it too abstract, and parents were mystified by the abrupt switch from the mathematics they knew. Because of the volume of criticism, the new math was removed from the schools by the early 1970s. See also **fuzzy math; Mathematically Correct; math wars; new new math; whole math**.

---

new new math: A derogatory term referring to the applied mathematics and discovery methods promoted in the national standards for school mathematics published by the National Council of Teachers of Mathematics (NCTM) in 1989. NCTM was widely applauded for being the first national organization to establish voluntary national standards for its subject, but critics complained that NCTM math ignored the teaching of basic skills while emphasizing that math problems could be solved in multiple ways and had no right or wrong answers. Exchanges between advocates and critics of NCTM math in the 1990s were described as the "math wars." See also **fuzzy math; Mathematically Correct; math wars; new math; whole math**.

Nickleby: A shorthand term referring to the federal No Child Left Behind (NCLB) legislation, meant to disparage the legislation's annual testing requirement and its accountability provisions.

No Child Left Behind Act (NCLB): The reauthorization of the Elementary and Secondary Education Act, which was originally passed in 1965 as part of President Lyndon B. Johnson's Great Society program. NCLB was passed in fall 2001 and signed into law in early 2002. It represents a significant change in the federal government's role in public schools throughout the United States, particularly in terms of assessment, accountability, and teacher quality. The law requires states to annually test all students from grades 3 to 8 in reading and mathematics (and in science in 2007–2008) and to disaggregate their scores by race, disability, and other factors. It requires states and districts to improve the achievement of disadvantaged pupils, including English language learners and students who live in poverty. NCLB also provides funding for innovative programs and supports the right of parents to transfer their children to a different public school if their school is low-performing or unsafe. Schools and districts are supposed to achieve a goal of 100 percent proficiency in reading and mathematics for every subgroup by the 2013–2014 school year. Critics complain that the law has led to an overemphasis on testing and narrowed the focus of the curriculum to only the tested subjects; that its goal of 100 percent proficiency is unattainable; that it has federalized education policy; and that its sanctions and remedies are ineffectual. Defenders of the law say that it has brought needed attention to students who were previously neglected because their low scores were buried in average school and district performance. See also **Elementary and Secondary Education Act (ESEA)**.

nonsectarian: Having no religious affiliation.

normal curve: A bell-shaped distribution of test scores showing that most students score near the average and that relatively few score much higher or much lower than average. See also **bell curve; grading on the curve**.

normal distribution: A distribution of scores or other measures that in graphic form has a distinctive bell-shaped appearance. In a normal distribution, the measures are distributed symmetrically around the mean. Cases are concentrated near the mean and decrease in frequency, according to a precise mathematical equation, the farther one departs from the mean. The assumption that many mental and psychological characteristics are distributed normally has been very important in test development. See also **bell curve; normal curve**.

normed score: A score that compares the performance of an individual student with the performance of a nationally representative group of students of the same age or grade.

norm-referenced test (NRT): A standardized test designed to compare the scores of individuals or groups of individuals with the scores achieved by a representative sample of individuals with similar characteristics, members of a so-called reference group. Norm-referenced tests are useful for comparing the performance of students in one school, district, county, state, or nation with the performance of students in other schools, districts, counties, states, or nations. Norms are averages, not standards; they show how students actually perform, not how they should perform. Most standardized tests are norm-referenced. Contrast **criterion-referenced test (CRT)**.

norms: The distribution of test scores of some specified group, called the norm group. For example, the norm could consist of a national sample of all 4th graders, a national sample of all 4th grade males, or perhaps all 4th graders in some local district.

norms versus standards: The distinction between norms and standards. Norms are indicators of what students know and can do. They represent an average of current overall achievement; if achievement is low, the norms will reflect the status quo, offering no judgment about whether achievement should be higher. Standards, on the other hand, are arbitrary but considered judgments of what students—with appropriate instruction, resources, and motivation—*should* know and be able to do, given a set of test items.

no-stakes test: A test whose results are not released to students or their teachers and that thus has no consequences at all. The National Assessment of Educational Progress, which tests national and state samples of students, is a no-stakes test because no individual student ever learns his or her score, and no action is taken on the basis of his or her test performance. Student performance is reported for the nation, for the state, and, in a few instances, for cities, but not for individual students. See also **low-stakes test**. Contrast **high-stakes test**.

noticings: Observations or comments by a teacher or a student about student activities, often found in balanced literacy classes. A teacher may be asked by a supervisor to create a list of "our noticings" about the quality of student work in the classroom.

objectives: Stated desirable outcomes of instruction.

off-the-shelf tests: Professionally prepared tests used without modifications. Off-the-shelf tests are ready-made standardized tests that are purchased by a school, district, or state from test publishers, as opposed to tests that are custom-made to match the standards and specifications of the school, district, or state.

one size fits all: A phrase intended to disparage efforts either to develop or to impose a common curriculum or a uniform pedagogy on school systems.

open education movement: An innovation of the late 1960s and the early 1970s that created student-centered schools. In one version of the open education approach, the walls between classrooms were removed so that three or four classes of students shared the same space; some schools were built with fewer walls to support this approach. In another version, students were free to move around the classroom and choose from among a variety of activity centers, with minimal direction from the teacher. For a decade or so, the movement was a sensation and seemed to sweep the world of education. By the late 1970s, there was a public reaction against the open education movement because of negative evaluations and complaints about lack of student discipline. Walls were restored where they had been removed and added where they had never existed. By the 1980s, the open education movement had waned, although the spirit that animated it remains a hardy perennial in American education.

open-ended question: A question that allows students to give an answer in their own language and that does not have a single correct answer, such as an essay question.

open-response item: A question on a standardized test that requires the test taker to write the answer in his or her own words rather than choose the right answer from a list, as in a multiple-choice question. Also called *independent-response item*. See also **constructed-response item.** Contrast **closed-response item.**

opportunity to learn (OTL): The standards that measure the extent to which key education resources—such as experienced teachers, adequate resources, and a rich curriculum—are provided at a school site or in a district or state. In the broadest sense, providing opportunity to learn means fostering learning and development by making up the difference between the resources available to the most and the least privileged students.

oral reading: Reading out loud. In the public schools of the 19th century and the early decades of the 20th century, oral reading was an important class exercise. In the 1920s, however, researchers decided that oral reading was undesirable after comparing the eye movements of students who were reading out loud with those of students who were reading silently. Because students who read silently were reading faster than those who read out loud, the experts decided that reading aloud was inefficient and accordingly advised teachers to encourage silent reading and to discourage oral reading. Some even warned parents not to read aloud to their children because it would teach them to learn through their ears instead of their eyes. Part of this hostility toward oral reading stemmed from its relationship to phonetics, which stressed the relationship between letters and sounds. Reading aloud increased students' awareness of the importance

of the sounds made by different letters and combinations of letters, but when they read silently, the sounds were unimportant.
None of this research would be recognized today as credible, but
the negative attitudes among educators against phonetics and
oral reading persisted for many years. Contrast **silent reading**.

outcome-based education (OBE): A controversial offshoot of
the standards movement in the 1990s that focused on such outcomes as students' attitudes, behaviors, values, and skills, with
the goal of preparing them for everyday life and the needs of the
workplace. Critics of outcome-based education objected to this
approach on grounds that it was a far cry from academic standards and that it inappropriately intruded into students' personal lives. Advocates defended OBE, saying that it was a
necessary response to the individual needs of students. Heated
political controversies swirled around outcome-based education, especially in Pennsylvania and Ohio, and in most places it
was eventually abandoned.

outside-in reforms: Reforms—such as standards, tests, mandates, and regulations—that are imposed on the school by an
outside government agency. Contrast **inside-out reforms**.

Outward Bound: A nonprofit educational organization that seeks
to inspire motivation and character development in students
through expeditions and adventures in the outdoors, where they
learn self-reliance, practice teamwork, and engage in various
activities. Outward Bound sponsors Expeditionary Learning
Schools in districts around the United States.

pacing chart: A graphic representation of time on task that describes what students and teachers will be doing during a course of study. The pacing chart is a customized guide that some teachers use to plan instruction in each subject and to ensure that they teach the essential skills and knowledge of each topic within a specified period of time while meeting the requirements of state standards.

Paideia Program: An approach to teaching developed by philosopher Mortimer Adler that combines coaching, lecturing, and Socratic dialogue as teaching methods to encourage deep thinking about such traditional subjects as literature, mathematics, science, and the performing arts. Adler's *Paideia Proposal*, *Paideia Program*, and *Paideia Problems and Possibilities* are rooted in the social, political, and educational philosophy of Aristotle. See also **Adler, Mortimer J. (1902–2001); Socratic seminar**.

paradigm: A pattern or an example. Also, a large philosophical framework or way of thinking that deeply influences assumptions, decisions, policies, and actions.

paraprofessional: A trained aide who assists the classroom teacher, often in special education classes. The "para" does not have the same credentials and training as the regular classroom teacher. Also called *para-educator*.

parent engagement: The involvement of parents in the daily lives and schooling of their children. Parents who are actively involved with their children read to them, share family stories with them, listen to their concerns, check their homework, meet with their teachers, and make sure that they are properly supervised when they are not in school.

parent/school compact: Under No Child Left Behind, a written agreement of shared responsibility that defines the goals and expectations of schools and parents as partners in the effort to improve student achievement.

Parent Teacher Association (PTA): A voluntary organization that brings together parents, teachers, and other interested persons in a particular school or school district, usually to raise funds, build parental involvement at school, and conduct other activities to promote the welfare of the school. The term *PTA* refers officially to groups affiliated with the National PTA; the generic term *PTO* (parent teacher organization) encompasses all parent-teacher groups, regardless of their affiliation. PTAs and PTOs are normally parent-dominated and rely on voluntary participation.

Parker, Francis W. (1837–1902): A pioneer of the progressive education movement. A native of New Hampshire, Parker served in the U.S. Civil War, where he rose to the rank of colonel and was known ever after as Colonel Parker. After the war he traveled extensively in Europe, where he learned about the new pedagogical ideas of such theorists as Rousseau, Froebel, Pestalozzi, and Herbart. In 1875, he became superintendent of schools in Quincy, Massachusetts, where he put his ideas into practice. In place of traditional harsh discipline and rote memorization, he emphasized informal methods of instruction. Quincy's students excelled on state tests. He subsequently led the public schools in Boston and headed the Cook County Normal School in Chicago. Although less well known than John Dewey, Parker was referred to by Dewey himself as the "father of progressive education."

parking lot: A term usually referring to the 9th grade, where many low-achieving students get stuck because they are unable to earn sufficient academic credits to move forward. This situation usually results from the promotion of middle school students who are unable to do 9th grade work.

partner reading: A technique sometimes used in bilingual classrooms that pairs an English language learner with a more experienced reader for help with part of a reading assignment.

pass/fail: A grading system in which the student either passes or fails, with no other grade possible.

passive compliance: Action on the part of a student to do what is expected but with no enthusiasm and a minimum of effort.

pedagogue: A person with an advanced degree in education who works as a teacher, an administrator, or a professor of education. The term has pejorative connotations, suggesting someone who is pedantic or dull.

pedagogy: The study of education and education practice. Also, a philosophy about the best way to teach. Pedagogy is not the same as curriculum: whereas curriculum details *what* to teach, pedagogy details *how* to teach. Most states mandate what will be taught in the public schools but leave judgments of how to teach to teachers, knowing that there is no single way that is best in every situation. In addition to *how* to teach, the study of pedagogy should address the deeper moral and philosophical question of *why* to teach.

peer-based program: A program in which students teach other students of the same age.

peer coaching: A process in which teachers visit one another's classes to observe instruction and offer feedback.

peer culture: The norms and values of a group that influence the behavior and attitudes of the group's members, as well as those who want to be part of the group or to be admired by the group. In secondary school, peer culture has a large effect on how students behave, what they aspire to, and what they care about. A peer culture that values athletics, good looks, and popularity often devalues academic success. Schools must be aware of students' peer culture and make concerted efforts to establish a climate in which students value learning, respect themselves and others, practice kindness, and aspire to pursue higher education and to be good citizens. See also **peer pressure**.

peer evaluation: Evaluation by peers, whether of a student by another student or of a teacher by another teacher.

peer intervention: A peer assistance program in which successful teachers help struggling colleagues develop professionally and address instructional issues.

peer mediation: A program that trains students to resolve conflicts between other students or between groups of students. See also **conflict resolution instruction**.

peer pressure: The subtle but strong influence that a group has on the behavior of individuals who want to be accepted or admired by the group. If "everyone is doing it," then a student may feel compelled to go along with whatever it is to be accepted by others of his or her age. When everyone is doing something that is harmful to themselves or others—like indulging in drugs or alcohol or harassing others—peer pressure can have a deeply negative effect on adolescent development. It takes maturity and a strong sense of individualism to resist peer pressure. See also **peer culture**.

peer resource programs: Programs that train students to provide their peers with counseling, education, and support on such issues as prejudice, drugs, violence, child abuse, dropping out, AIDS, and peer pressure. Students are also trained to provide tutoring and conflict mediation.

peer review: In education, programs in which teachers evaluate and advise other teachers who are struggling to succeed. Peer review programs have been supported in various locales by the

National Education Association and the American Federation of Teachers. The recipients of peer review may be new teachers or tenured teachers who are floundering in their classrooms. A decision to remove a teacher or to counsel him or her to leave the profession would be reached only as a last option after all forms of counseling and mentoring have been tried. In publishing, peer review refers to the evaluation of articles by people who are knowledgeable in the same field of study. In government, peer review by qualified experts is often used to make informed and nonpolitical decisions about the award of grants and contracts.

peer tutoring: A program in which one student helps another student in the same grade learn material in which the first is more proficient.

Pell Grants: Federal grants that provide tuition assistance for low-income college students, named for the late Senator Claiborne Pell of Rhode Island, who championed the program.

performance assessment: A test that requires students to perform a task rather than to select a correct answer from a list of possible responses. Examples of performance assessments include essay questions, portfolios, and demonstrations. Students may be required to perform such tasks as serving a volleyball, solving a particular type of mathematics problem, or writing a short business letter to inquire about a product. Sometimes the task assesses the student's ability to apply knowledge learned in school. For example, a student might be asked to determine what types of plants could be grown in various soil samples by measuring their pH levels.

performance-based: A descriptor of any program, assessment, or activity that emphasizes students doing something (such as creating a science project or writing a history essay) as opposed to listening to the teacher or answering multiple-choice test questions.

performance incentive: Any reward, monetary or other, used to encourage teachers, administrators, or other school staff to increase the academic achievement of their students. See also **bonus pay; incentives for teachers; merit pay**.

performance standards: Standards that describe how well students should be expected to master the content standards. For example, whereas content standards may say that all 8th graders should take Algebra I, performance standards would say what level of mastery of Algebra I is necessary for promotion to the next grade (or for achievement with honors). See also **content standards**.

permissiveness: An attitude or a policy that grants a large degree of freedom to students to make their own choices. Such an attitude or policy is reflected in a school's rules and expectations, or lack thereof; it may extend not only to student behavior in class or school but also to allowing students to decide what to learn and what courses to take.

Perry Preschool Project: A longitudinal study that examined the lives of 123 African American children born in poverty and at high risk of school failure. From 1962 to 1967, at ages 3 and 4, the subjects were randomly divided into a program group that received a high-quality preschool program and a comparison group that received no preschool program. Those who participated in the high-quality preschool program were later found to have higher earnings, to be more likely to be employed, to be less likely to have committed crimes, and to be more likely to have graduated from high school than were adults from the comparison group who had received no preschool education.

Pestalozzi, Johann Heinrich (1746–1827): A Swiss education reformer whose theories deeply influenced the development of elementary education in Europe and the United States. The schools established by Pestalozzi in Switzerland attracted wide attention. Opposed to the customary reliance on strict discipline and rote memorization, he favored an approach based on kindness and understanding of the child's world. He believed that education should be based on concrete experiences, so he introduced the use of tactile objects to teach natural science to children. He emphasized both the moral and the intellectual aspects of education, as well as the importance of well-educated teachers. A lifelong social reformer, Pestalozzi believed that good education could change society for the better.

phoneme: Any minimal unit of sound that is used to distinguish between words in a language—that is, the vowels and consonants (and other elements, such as glottal stops, clicks, or tones) that serve to distinguish words from one another in a language. Thus, the /p/ and /b/ in *pat* and *bat* are phonemes of English because the distinction between them is sufficient to distinguish the one word from the other.

phonemic awareness: The ability to recognize that words and syllables are composed of bits of sound (phonemes), which is important in learning to read.

phonemic sequencing error: A type of mistake that occurs when a student is unable to put sounds together in the right order to understand the meaning of a word or phrase.

phonics: Any of a number of approaches to teaching students the alphabetic code of a language—that is, how the sounds of the language are encoded into writing and then decoded during reading. Instruction in phonics teaches beginning readers the relationships between letters and sounds and shows them how to decode words by sounding them out. See also **alphabet**.

phonological awareness: Awareness of the sounds of language and of various aspects of language sounds, such as stress and intonation.

phonological delay: A lag in a student's ability to understand and produce sounds, causing him or her problems in reading, spelling, and speaking.

physical education: Classes in which students exercise and learn to play sports. Also known as *gym*. See also **physical welfare**.

physical welfare: Physical education class, with an emphasis on health and well-being rather than competitive sports. Also called *kinetic wellness*. See also **physical education**.

pie chart: A chart that is used to show the percentage or absolute number of each of several distinct elements of a whole; also called a *circle graph*. As an example, one might create a pie chart by drawing a circle; labeling it "Students at Abraham Lincoln High School"; and dividing the circle into pie-slice sections labeled "Asian American," "African American," "Hispanic American," "European American," and "Other." The sizes of the sections should reflect the relative percentages of the groups in the school's student population.

pilot test: A trial run of a standardized test used to obtain information regarding the test's clarity, difficulty, validity, reliability, time requirements, and administrative requirements. Pilot testing is often used to help test makers revise and select the items that will appear in an assessment.

plagiarism: A form of academic theft, stealing someone else's words and trying to pass them off as one's own. For example, copying a portion of a book or an essay from the Internet and submitting it to the teacher as one's own work is plagiarism. When students copy someone else's language and include it in their own work, they must put the copied language into quotation marks and insert a footnote identifying the original source of the material. If the source is identified in the student's work, quotation marks and a footnote may not be necessary.

planful: In a carefully considered, or planned, manner.

planning period: A period set aside for teachers to plan lessons, meet with parents, and evaluate student work.

Plessy v. Ferguson: An 1896 U.S. Supreme Court decision that is the source of the phrase "separate but equal." It upheld a Louisiana law that segregated rail passengers by race, with separate cars for whites and blacks. Seven of the eight justices held that so long as the facilities were equal, then there was nothing wrong with state-imposed racial segregation. Only one justice, John Marshall Harlan, dissented. He argued that the states did not have the power to regulate their citizens solely on the basis of their race. In a memorable passage, Harlan wrote that "in view of the Constitution, in the eye of the law, there is in this country no superior, dominant, ruling class of citizens. There is no caste here. Our Constitution is color-blind, and neither knows nor tolerates classes among citizens. In respect of civil rights, all citizens are equal before the law." The *Plessy* decision supported racial segregation in public facilities, including schools, until 1954, when the Court issued its *Brown v. Board of Education* decision rejecting "separate but equal" as unconstitutional. See also **Brown v. Board of Education**.

pod: A group of students. In some programs, a pod means students who have been identified on the basis of their ability and good behavior; in others, a pod refers to students randomly selected to engage in inquiry activities.

portable classrooms: Temporary classrooms, often set up in mobile trailers, meant to relieve overcrowding in the main building. Districts use portable classrooms when enrollment grows rapidly or when class size is reduced, both factors that create a need for additional classrooms. Portable classrooms are less costly than new buildings and supply classroom space while new buildings are under construction. Also called *learning cottages*. See also **classroom trailers**.

portfolio assessment: An alternative form of assessment in which the teacher reviews a body of student work collected throughout a course or school year to evaluate the student's performance over time. Grades are based in whole or in part on this packet of materials, which demonstrates the progress of the student's knowledge and skills and often includes some form of self-reflection by the student. A student portfolio assessment can include writing samples, examples of how the student solved mathematics problems, results of scientific experiments, and so on. Portfolio assessment is valuable for the individual classroom teacher but cannot be used to compare the work of students across a grade level, a school district, or a state.

postbaccalaureate: A program of further education or career preparation for students who have received their undergraduate degree.

postsecondary: A description of any program or activity that follows graduation from high school.

power standards: Efforts by state or district officials to identify the knowledge and skills that are absolutely essential for students to learn. Power standards are a subset of the complete list of standards for each grade and subject. They are the minimum fundamentals that every student should learn before advancing to the next grade.

Praxis: (1) Practical application of learning; habitual, customary practice of an art, a science, or a skill. (2) A series of tests prepared by the Educational Testing Service and used by many states for teaching licensing and certification. Praxis I measures basic academic skills of would-be teachers; Praxis II measures their general and subject-specific knowledge and teaching skills; and Praxis III assesses their classroom performance.

prayer in schools: A reference to the debate over whether prayer should be allowed in public schools. For many decades, most public schools began each day with a recitation of the Pledge of Allegiance, a patriotic song like the national anthem, and a short prayer or Bible reading. In 1962, the U.S. Supreme Court invalidated state laws that required prayer in the public schools in *Engel v. Vitale*. In this case, the Board of Regents of the state of New York had approved a nondenominational prayer that was to be recited at the beginning of each school day: "Almighty God, we acknowledge our dependence upon Thee, and we beg Thy blessing upon us, our parents, our teachers and our Country." The Court held that the prayer was religious and violated the Establishment Clause of the First Amendment to the U.S. Constitution. In 1963, the Court ruled that state-sponsored Bible reading in the public schools was unconstitutional. That case, called *Abington Township v. Schempp*, originated in Pennsylvania, where public school students were required to hear and read passages from the Bible each day. The Court held that the state violated the Constitution by compelling religious exercises in the public schools. The issue of prayer in schools continued to be controversial for many years afterward, and several states sought ways to circumvent these decisions.

prekindergarten: A program for children who are too young to enter kindergarten (usually 3 or 4 years old), designed to teach them social skills through activities and play; also called *preschool*. Just as kindergarten prepares children for 1st grade, prekindergarten prepares children for kindergarten. Because of the United States' great increase in the proportion of working mothers, public preschool programs for very young children have become increasingly popular with parents, especially those for whom private child care is too expensive. Head Start is a preschool program funded by the federal government for children from low-income families. In recent years, as research continues to suggest the value of such programs, a number of jurisdictions have begun planning or implementing universal preschool for all 4-year-old children, and in some cases, for younger children as well. See also **Head Start.**

prep period: Time set aside in the school day during which teachers can prepare for their classes or mark student papers.

preservice teacher education: A curriculum that is specifically designed for the preparation of teachers. This curriculum is "preservice" because intending teachers complete it prior to beginning their careers as classroom teachers. Preservice teacher education typically takes place in undergraduate programs, but it can be completed in graduate school as well. Preservice teacher education programs include coursework in subject matter, pedagogy, education psychology, and foundations (e.g., history and philosophy of education), as well as practice teaching assignments of various durations. See also **inservice teacher education.**

prewriting: A process of initiating or organizing ideas for a composition before starting the writing process.

primary source: An original, firsthand document, photograph, interview, set of data, record of an event, or other source of information that originates from the time being studied and that is often the basis for further study. Contrast **secondary source.**

print-rich environment: A classroom, home, or other location in which there are ample displays of written language, such as books, charts, magazines, signs, and student papers. Also known as a *literacy-rich environment*.

prior knowledge: The totality of an individual's experiences and knowledge at any given time—that is, what a student brings as background information to a new learning experience. The more prior knowledge a person has, the more prepared he or she will be to learn new ideas. Almost everything that a person learns or can learn depends on the extent of his or her prior knowledge. One of the major missions of school is to build students' fund of background knowledge so that they have a foundation for future learning.

private schools: Schools that are managed by an independent board of trustees or organization and sustained in whole or in part by the tuition of their students and their endowment, if any. Private schools may be sectarian or nonsectarian. They are usually, but not always, exempt from most of the state and federal regulations that pertain to public schools.

privatization: The result of a decision by public officials to relinquish control of certain functions in the public sector to private organizations. So, for example, a decision by a local school board to replace its custodians with a private contractor would be an example of privatization, as would a decision to replace the cafeteria staff with a private catering firm to supply lunches to students. Similarly, turning control of public schools over to nonpublic agencies, be they for-profit or nonprofit, is a form of privatization.

process approach to reading and writing: A method of teaching reading and writing that stresses the process of learning these skills. Reading teachers may concern themselves less with the accuracy of students' reading than with students' processes of responding, reacting, asking questions, comparing text with self, and applying other comprehension strategies. Similarly, writing teachers may disregard the grammatical accuracy of student essays but pay a great deal of attention to the care with which students plan their essays, draft them, revise them, respond to teacher feedback, edit them again, and share or publish them. The process writing approach combines a number of instructional activities to teach writing, including extended writing opportunities, writing for real audiences, one-to-one instruction, and cycles of writing.

professional development: Training intended to teach teachers or administrators the knowledge and skills they need to perform their jobs well. Often, these programs are aimed at veteran teachers to help them update their professional skills and knowledge.

professional period: Time during the school day that is set aside for teachers to give help to or get help from other teachers.

proficiency: Mastery of skills and knowledge for a specific grade or subject.

proficient: One of three achievement levels on the federally funded National Assessment of Educational Progress and on many state tests. *Proficient* represents solid academic performance. See also **achievement levels; advanced; basic.**

Program Improvement (PI): An intervention mandated by the No Child Left Behind Act (NCLB). When a school or a district that receives federal Title I funds fails to make adequate yearly progress (AYP) toward having all students proficient in reading and mathematics by the 2013–2014 school year, that school or district then enters Program Improvement status. This label means the school or district is in need of improvement. Each state, with federal approval, sets goals for AYP each year. Once a school makes AYP for two years in a row, it can leave Program Improvement status. NCLB lists a series of increasingly onerous interventions for schools that remain in Program Improvement. These begin with giving parents the option to transfer their children to a school that is not in Program Improvement, with transportation provided. In the next year, the school must provide professional development to teachers and staff and offer extra tutoring to students from low-income families. Over time, a school that continues to fail to meet its goals for adequate yearly progress will face significant restructuring, such as dismissal of the staff, takeover by the state or by private contractors, or conversion to charter status.

programmed learning: A learning technique in which lessons, usually delivered by computer, are carefully detailed in a script. The lessons are based on step-by-step behavioral objectives. At every step, students are assessed for mastery of the material; depending on their performance, they may go back a few steps or advance to more demanding work. The goal is to make sure that students learn precisely the material that has been entered into the program and that their learning is not derailed by incompetent or ineffective teaching. Some teachers object to programmed learning because it is a rigid system and is designed to be "teacher-proof." See also **teacher-proof curriculum**.

progressive education: A philosophy of education that promotes active, experiential learning, as opposed to learning solely from books, lectures, recitation, and practice. A complete definition of progressive education could, and indeed has, taken up a book by itself. Some associate progressive education with the provision of social and medical services in schools; others think of it as a bridge between school and society; and still others relate it to political radicalism. Mostly, it is associated with child-centered education that is based on children's interests and concerns. The major philosopher of progressive education was John Dewey. Others include William Heard Kilpatrick and Boyd Bode. See also **child-centered education; Dewey, John (1859–1962); Kilpatrick, William Heard (1871–1965)**.

Project 2061: A reform proposal by the American Association for the Advancement of Science to improve the quality of education in mathematics, science, and technology by the year 2061.

project-based learning: A teaching technique in which students learn by doing, engaging in activities that lead to the creation of products based on their own experiences. The project method was first described in 1918 by William Heard Kilpatrick of Teachers College, Columbia University, who hoped to replace subject-matter teaching with real-life projects chosen by students.

Project STAR (Student/Teacher Achievement Ratio): A four-year longitudinal study on the effects of reducing class size, funded by the state of Tennessee. The study found that primary-grade students (especially black students) in small classes of 13–17 students learned more reading and math than did comparable groups of students in regular classes of 22–25 students.

promotion: Advancement of a student from one grade to the next grade. See also **social promotion**. Contrast **retention**.

prompt: Directions given as part of a constructed-response test item. The term is used most commonly to describe directions for a written response—in such cases, it is called a *writing prompt* or an *essay prompt*—but also refers to document-based questions on social studies tests that require an extended response (e.g., writing an essay, generating a list, or drawing a map).

Proposition 227: An initiative statute passed by voters in California in 1998 to restrict bilingual education by requiring all public school instruction to be conducted in English.

protected meeting time: A block of time that is reserved for a regularly scheduled meeting.

protected monopoly: A description of public education used by critics who believe that public schools perform poorly because they are a state monopoly that is shielded from competition and market forces. Such critics also maintain that the relationship between teachers' unions and school boards further strengthens the monopoly because boards are often elected or selected with the support of the unions with which they negotiate.

protocol: A procedure for doing something—for example, for conducting a particular test, organizing a meeting, or analyzing student work. Also, a self-report of what one is thinking, doing, or feeling at each step in the process of completing some activity.

psychometrician: A testing expert; someone who has earned an advanced degree in the area of assessment and statistics and knows how to develop and analyze tests that are used in schools or in the workplace.

public engagement: Involvement of the general public in discussion of school-related issues.

public schools: Schools that are supported by the state and thus are subject to state laws and regulations and charge no tuition. Most public schools are open to all, but a relatively small number of specialized public schools require students to pass qualifying admissions examinations.

pullout program: A Title I–funded activity intended to help low-performing students by removing them from their regular classes to give them additional instruction. The reason for taking students out of their regular classes is to ensure that they are getting the extra instruction that federal dollars pay for. Critics complained that students in pullout programs are likely to fall further behind their peers because they miss regular class time. In response to critics, federal laws were changed to allow the extra federal dollars to be spent on entire schools for schoolwide programs, despite the likelihood that many students who need extra instruction may no longer get it. See also **Elementary and Secondary Education Act (ESEA); schoolwide program; Title I**. Contrast **push-in program**.

pupil-teacher ratio: The total student enrollment divided by the number of full-time equivalent teachers. This ratio is usually smaller than average class size because some teachers, such as reading specialists, work outside the regular classroom. The pupil-teacher ratio is the most common statistic used for comparing data across states. See also **average class size**.

push-in program: A program in which a teacher of a specific population of students (for example, gifted students or bilingual students) visits their general education classroom on a regular basis to give them additional instruction. Contrast **pullout program**.

p-value: A statistical concept that describes the difficulty level of a test item, determined by testing students to find out how the item works in reality. The p-value falls between 1.0 and 0.0 and is calculated by dividing the number of students who answered an item correctly by the total number of students who attempted to answer the item. An item with a p-value of 1.0 is very easy because everyone got it right, and an item with a p-value of 0.0 is very hard because no one got it right. Knowledge of test items' p-value can be used to manipulate test scores; for example, a test maker can increase the proportion of easy (high p-value) questions to make test scores go up, even though students are not learning any more than in the past.

Pygmalion effect: The tendency of a student to perform in accordance with the teacher's expectations. According to this theory, if a teacher tells a student that he or she is gifted, the student's achievement will rise remarkably. Conversely, if the teacher tells the student that he or she is not very smart, the student's achievement will falter. Although many people believe in the Pygmalion effect, attempts to demonstrate its validity have met with poor results.

qualitative evaluation: An assessment that employs observations and impressions to evaluate the performance of the target of assessment—for example, an education program, an education institution, school staff, or a group of students. Qualitative evaluations often generate detailed information on unanticipated phenomena and yield insights into how outcomes occurred. Qualitative information may be time-consuming to gather and summarize, and qualitative evaluation may be more subjective than quantitative evaluation. Qualitative analysis is often employed in formative evaluation, which focuses on ongoing diagnosis and improvement. Contrast **quantitative evaluation**.

quantitative evaluation: A method of assessment that evaluates performance using objective systematic observations, rating scales, and paper-and-pencil tests and questionnaires that yield numerical information for statistical analysis. Quantitative evaluations are often used to assess the value of education institutions and projects and the accomplishments of students and staff. Contrast **qualitative evaluation**.

randomized field trials: An experimental technique that randomly assigns matched groups either to an experimental treatment or to no treatment at all. This random allocation ensures that the two groups being compared do not differ in ways that would affect their response to a given treatment. Randomized field trials generate solid evidence about the relative effectiveness of various interventions and are considered the gold standard of research.

raw score: The number of questions answered correctly on a test, particularly a multiple-choice test. Because the test questions do not all have the same level of difficulty, this information is of limited use for evaluative purposes. In addition, such scores are generally not comparable from one test to another because the number and difficulty of the questions vary. For this reason, raw scores are often expressed as norm-referenced percentiles or criterion-referenced categories.

read-aloud: A classroom activity in which students are read to by a teacher, a classroom aide, or other students. The students may listen as a whole class or in small groups. Read-alouds are supposed to teach students skills in reading comprehension, listening, and critical thinking, as well as to improve their attitudes toward reading.

---

reader-response theory: A theory of reading propounded in 1938 by educator and researcher Louise Rosenblatt asserting that the meaning of a text is not static, but an active construction that depends on the reader's reaction to the text and his or her personal attitudes, feelings, and experiences. Reader-response theorists assert that readers construct texts in the act of reading and that a given text has no meaning in and of itself but rather has as many meanings as there are readers and readings. Critics complain that the theory implies that a student's feelings about a work of literature are more important than the author's purposes.

---

reading in the content areas: A phrase referring to the belief that reading instruction is the responsibility of all teachers, including those in the various academic subject areas, such as history, science, and mathematics. Proponents believe that it is vital for content-area teachers to teach reading as well as their subjects because so many secondary students have poor reading skills. Critics worry that high school students will be cheated of instructional time in the academic subjects while their teachers are trying to teach reading. Also called *reading across the curriculum*.

Reading Recovery: An individualized reading skills intervention program for students who are having difficulty learning to read. Reading Recovery teachers are trained in a yearlong course that integrates reading, writing, and listening techniques.

---

realia: Objects from "real life" used for classroom instruction, such as coins, tools, games, toys, and other physical manifestations of the world outside school. Realia do not include books or periodicals.

---

real world: A term used in the education field to refer to the world outside school. Many people think of the learning done in school as theoretical rather than "real." However, academic learning is an investment in human capital that will likely reap greater returns in the long run than immediate real-world experience. School teaches students to understand symbolic representation and to generalize from particulars to principles. This knowledge enables the learner to benefit from the accumulated experience of others, not just from his or her own personal experience.

recess: In elementary school, free time for play.

reciprocal accountability: Educators' shared responsibility to provide the same degree of help to their peers that they themselves receive.

reciprocal learning: A pedagogical strategy in which students help one another to master skills or concepts presented by the teacher. Generally, students work in pairs and take turns acting as coach.

reconstitution: A drastic corrective action for a school where students have performed poorly for several years with no sign of improvement. Typically, a reconstitution involves the replacement of most or all of the school's staff and faculty and the hiring of a new principal.

reflection: The process of thinking about what one is doing or what one has just finished doing. For example, students may be encouraged to reflect on their writing, and teachers to reflect on their practice. Reflection on one's behavior and efforts should involve self-critique, self-analysis, and self-evaluation. However, the term today is often misunderstood to mean reflecting on one's feelings rather than engaging in any sort of critical self-assessment.

reflection room: A place in school where disruptive students are sent for a time-out to think about their misbehavior. Also known as *reinforcement room*. See also **alternative instruction room; detention**.

reflective practitioner: An educator who thinks about the art and craft of teaching, ponders the rationale for teaching, reviews what he or she has been doing in the classroom, and analyzes whether or not it was successful. Unfortunately, the term has become a cliché signaling only that the teacher has learned to parrot the language that he or she has heard in professional development sessions.

Regional Educational Laboratory Program: A federally funded network of 10 organizations across the United States that conduct research and evaluations of educational programs and disseminate information in the regions they serve. The regional laboratories were established by the U.S. Congress in 1965 as part of the Elementary and Secondary Education Act. Every five years, there is a competitive process in which some are renewed for another term and some are replaced.

Rehabilitation Act of 1973 (Section 504): A federal law stating that no qualified person shall, on the basis of a disability, be excluded from participation in, be denied the benefits of, or be subjected to discrimination by employers, educational institutions, or any program or activity that receives or benefits from federal financial assistance. Section 504 defines an "individual with a handicap" more broadly than does the Individuals with Disabilities Education Act (IDEA), and in some circumstances provides additional rights not available under IDEA. The Office for Civil Rights (OCR) of the U.S. Department of Education enforces this law for all elementary, secondary, and post-secondary schools. The OCR prohibits specific discriminatory activities, such as the assignment of students with disabilities to segregated classes or facilities. In elementary and secondary schools, students with disabilities may be assigned to separate facilities or courses only when such placement is necessary to provide them equal educational opportunity and when the separate facilities and services are comparable to other facilities and services.

released time: Time set aside in the public school day when students are permitted to leave school grounds to receive religious instruction. Some states permit it; others do not. Schools that provide released time may not encourage or discourage participation, penalize those who do not participate, or allow religious instruction by outsiders on school premises during the school day.

relevant: An adjective usually attached to an activity or reading assignment to show that it has some relationship to students' own lives. Relevance has become very important in modern education, on the assumption that students want to learn mostly about ideas, events, and processes that they can connect to their personal experiences. The belief that whatever is studied must relate directly to students' own lives ignores the fact that students need extensive background knowledge on which to build new understandings. If students learn only what is directly connected to their own lives, their universe of learning will be severely limited and dependent on their family and community resources.

reliability: In testing, a measure of consistency. For example, if a person took different forms of the same test on two different days, scores on both tests should be similar. See also **fairness; validity**

religious schools: Schools operated by sectarian organizations and usually teaching the precepts of the religions that sponsor them. By law, public schools are not permitted to teach sectarian doctrines or to promote particular religious beliefs. Religious schools are also called *sectarian schools*. Contrast **secular schools**.

remedial education: Instruction or coaching intended to help students who have fallen behind in their studies to catch up or improve their skills.

report card: A written report to students and their parents or guardians, issued on a regular basis, about the students' progress in school. The report card may include grades, test scores, an attendance record, judgments about the student's behavior, and evaluative comments.

research-based: A descriptor of a program or policy that relies on credible, long-term studies of its effectiveness in practice. The best research uses randomized field trials, in which one group is randomly selected to receive the experimental treatment and a matched group does not receive it.

research shows . . . : A phrase often used to evoke authority and end discussions even when research is equivocal. Parents and other noneducators must be wary of accepting the claim that "research shows" a given outcome unless they receive a clear, impartial summary of the evidence.

resource room: A room where students (usually in special education) who need extra help with their work may go during regular class time. The resource room teacher may have special education and/or bilingual credentials and may provide one-on-one instruction or teach a subject to the students as a group. See also **learning lab**.

resource specialists: Specially credentialed teachers who give special education students extra help, either in regular classes or in a resource room.

restructuring: A term that signifies the redesign of a school, whether voluntary or involuntary. Schools voluntarily go through the restructuring process for a variety of reasons. A school may, for example, wish to provide a wider range of services to students and their families; to share decision-making authority with teachers, parents, and members of the local community; or to make changes in accordance with a new governance structure. Involuntary restructuring, on the other hand, may occur as a sanction for years of failure, as mandated by the No Child Left Behind Act. It could mean removing the principal and most or all of the staff, converting the school to a charter school, or turning over management of the school to the state or to a private contractor.

retention: The act or policy of holding students back from advancing to the next grade level if they do not meet established performance standards. Contrast **promotion; social promotion**.

return sweep: A description of the eye movements of a beginning reader as he or she moves from reading one line of print to the next.

reverse mainstreaming: The inclusion of students without disabilities as members of a class containing students who do have disabilities.

rigorous: Academically challenging.

Ritalin: A medicine containing methylphenidate, a central nervous system stimulant, that is sometimes prescribed for students who have been diagnosed with attention deficit/hyperactivity disorder. Ritalin is prescribed for students who have trouble paying attention and sitting still and is said to have a calming effect that enables students to concentrate on tasks. Boys are four times more likely than girls to be given the drug. Critics worry about the possible side effects of Ritalin, as well as about the general overmedication of children today. See also **attention deficit disorder (ADD).**

role model: A person whose conduct and achievements are exemplary and whose life is an inspiration for young people. A role model could be a national hero, a community leader, or a respected family friend.

rote learning: A learning technique that requires students to commit certain procedures or facts—for example, the multiplication tables—to memory. Frequently, students are expected to recite what they have memorized out loud, to show that they can recall and replicate what they learned by rote; this is called *drill.* Repetition is important in rote learning because it reinforces automaticity (e.g., the ability to know instantly that 7 x 7 = 49 without stopping to think about it). Critics of memorization and drill see rote learning as the epitome of bad education, but such routines do have their uses. Memorizing procedures, for example, is a time-saver that frees students' minds for creative thinking. See also **memorization.**

Rousseau, Jean-Jacques (1712–1778): A major figure in Western philosophy, born in Geneva, Switzerland. Rousseau claimed that man was good by nature but corrupted by society. His major work on education was *Émile,* in which he described the upbringing of a young boy, with himself as the caretaker. Everything in Émile's life was to be free and natural, without social imposition or constraint. He was to be shielded from the necessity of learning to read or of learning anything unless he needed to learn it. In Émile's supposedly ideal education, book learning is unimportant. Rousseau's educational philosophy of naturalism, romanticism, and rebellion against social constraints deeply influenced the child-centered wing of the U.S. progressive education movement.

rubber room: A room to which teachers are assigned when they are removed from teaching, a temporary placement until someone decides either to restore them to teaching or to discipline them for an infraction.

rubric: A set of criteria for evaluating student work or scoring tests. Rubrics describe what work must look like to be considered excellent, satisfactory, or less than satisfactory. In particular, rubrics are needed to minimize subjective judgments of performance assessments and essays. See also **scoring guide**.

running record: Observation notes made by the teacher about a student's oral reading ability. The teacher identifies the student's errors (or miscues) and documents the student's progress or problems. By looking at the running record, the teacher can analyze the type of reading and instruction that is best suited for the student.

sage on the stage: The teacher as someone who stands in front of the class, sharing his or her wisdom and knowledge. In current pedagogical parlance, the teacher should be "a guide on the side, not a sage on the stage." The ideal teacher is thus someone who facilitates learning and guides students as individuals and in small groups—not a deliverer of lectures. Contrast **guide on the side**.

San Antonio Independent School District v. Rodriguez: A 1973 U.S. Supreme Court decision ruling that large inequities in school financing among school districts within Texas did not violate the U.S. Constitution. In the wake of the decision, proponents of school finance equalization carried their legal arguments to state courts, where they frequently prevailed based on the language in their state constitutions. Consequently, many states were required by state courts to redesign the financing of public education to provide greater equality of resource distribution among schools and districts within the state.

SAT: A test of verbal and mathematical reasoning skills developed by the Educational Testing Service as a college entrance examination. Many colleges and universities use SAT I results to compare the skills of student applicants and to predict their future academic success. (The SAT II consists of a number of single-subject exams that measure content knowledge and skill level.) When the SAT was first administered in 1926, its initials stood for Scholastic Aptitude Test. Later, because the word *aptitude* had negative connotations and linked the test to its origins in the IQ testing movement of the 1920s, the College Board changed the *A* to stand for *Assessment*. Eventually, the College Board did away with any acronyms: today, the test is simply known as the SAT. See also **ACT; College Board**.

Saxon math: A mathematics program that relies on explicit, incremental instruction. The series was created by John Saxon, a former mathematics teacher and U.S. Air Force officer who believed that he had found a superior way to teach mathematics, based on the step-by-step instruction that he had encountered in the military. Each day, students work on a limited number of concepts, solving problems until they have mastered each concept and then moving on to the next. Every new assignment is a cumulative review of previously studied materials. The Saxon textbooks are popular with homeschooling families and some charter schools, but are shunned by many public school districts because they do not teach discovery and inquiry methods.

---

scaffolding: Coaching or modeling provided by a teacher to increase students' likelihood of success as they develop new skills or learn new concepts. Scaffolding in education is analogous to scaffolding in construction: just as a building's scaffolding is a temporary framework that is withdrawn when the structure is strong enough to stand on its own, so too is scaffolding in the classroom removed when students achieve competence in the targeted area. In any classroom, the teacher's goal is to enable students to perform tasks on their own, with a minimum of adult aid. Effective scaffolding occurs when the teacher explains an assignment, brings the task to an appropriate level of difficulty, breaks the task into a doable sequence of operations, provides feedback, and helps students gain mastery of new knowledge. Good teachers have always employed scaffolding, even if they never heard of the term.

scaling up: Efforts to expand the implementation of an innovation or a program from one or a few schools to a large number of schools. Over the years, schools have proven notoriously resistant to scaling up—in some cases, because an innovative idea depended on a single charismatic leader; in others, because the expansion of the program was not as well funded as the original innovation. In still other cases, the innovation seemed to succeed only as long as it was new, with interest (and results) fading when the innovation became routinized.

schema: A mental representation or codification of one's experience that includes a particular way of perceiving and responding to complex situations. See also **prior knowledge**.

scholastic aptitude: The combination of native and acquired abilities needed for successful academic learning.

school-based decision making (SBDM): A plan that shifts decision-making authority and control of a school's operation from the school district to the individual school—usually to a school council composed of parents, teachers, and school administrators. The school council is empowered to choose new staff, allocate budget resources, and make other decisions that affect the daily life of the school. Also called *school-based management (SBM)*. See also **shared decision making (SDM); site-based decision making (SBDM)**.

school board: A locally elected or appointed group that is responsible for oversight of a public school district, setting fiscal, personnel, instructional, and student-related policies. The school board has the authority to hire and fire the district superintendent, approve the annual budget, and negotiate contracts with employee unions.

school district: A local public education agency directed by an elected or appointed school board that exists primarily to operate public schools.

school of education: An institution of higher education (undergraduate or graduate) that prepares future teachers, school administrators, and other education professionals. Most states require teachers to hold a degree from a school of education.

school report card: An annual report released by a school that discloses to parents and the general public a variety of information about the school, such as student test scores, teacher credentials, dropout rates, class sizes, and resources. School report cards are required as part of the No Child Left Behind Act.

school site council (SSC): A group of teachers, parents, administrators, and interested community members who work together to develop and monitor a school's improvement plan. The school site council is a legally required decision-making body for any school receiving federal funds.

schools without walls: Schools that deliver the majority of instruction to students in informal community settings rather than in school buildings. These schools, small in number, operate mainly in urban environments, where there are ample opportunities for students to learn in such nontraditional settings as libraries, businesses, and museums. Schools without walls tend to serve youth who have been unsuccessful in regular public schools.

school-to-work (STW) program: A program intended to help high school students prepare for and make choices about their future jobs. Most school-to-work programs are subsidized by federal and state funding. Such programs direct students to post–high school jobs in service occupations; they do not provide preparation for the professions, which require a college degree.

schoolwide program: A program that uses Title I money to support comprehensive school improvement efforts and to help all students, particularly low-achieving and at-risk students, meet state standards at particular schools. To qualify as a Title I schoolwide program, at least 40 percent of a school's students must be considered low-income. Schoolwide programs can provide Title I services to all the students in the school, regardless of income level, and have more flexibility than targeted assistance programs do in using Title I funds. For example, schools operating schoolwide programs can combine Title I funds with other federal, state, and local funding to finance a comprehensive approach to improving student achievement. See also **pullout program; targeted assistance program (TAP); Title I.**

school within a school (SWAS): A school model based on the decision by district officials to divide a large comprehensive high school into several smaller schools, each with its own principal and teaching staff, intended to provide students with a more engaging and productive learning atmosphere. Critics complain that the SWAS model results in competition among the small schools for facilities, fewer electives and advanced courses, diminished sports teams and activities, and tension among students from different schools in the same building. See also **minischool; small learning community (SLC).**

scientifically based research: Research that involves the application of rigorous, systematic, and objective procedures to obtain reliable and valid knowledge relevant to educational activities and programs. See also **reliability; validity.**

scientific management: A movement in the early decades of the 20th century to establish efficient procedures for teaching and managing a school, based on time and motion studies and calculations of the cost of teaching various subjects. Scientific management experts like John Franklin Bobbitt and W. W. Charters used such studies to reduce student enrollments in academic subjects like Latin and algebra, on the belief that they were not useful. Influenced by the studies of efficiency experts like Bobbitt and Charters, many districts increased their offerings of vocational subjects and decreased their offerings of foreign languages and advanced courses in mathematics and science. Much of what Bobbitt and Charters advocated was revived in the 1950s as the "life adjustment movement." See also **task-based instruction; Taylorism.**

scope and sequence: A chart that shows the content (scope) and the order of presentation (sequence) of a curriculum. This framework describes all or part of the curriculum from kindergarten through 12th grade.

scoring guide: Recommendations or instructions for evaluating student work. A scoring guide typically describes what is being assessed and helps the rater place the students' work on the scale provided. See also **rubric**.

---

scripted program: Any educational program that describes in close detail how to teach the material. Scripted programs may raise the level of teaching if they are akin to a good recipe; however, they are unlikely to succeed if they attempt to impose routines and methods that teachers find patronizing and disrespectful.

---

scrubbing: A process in which teachers regrade student essays on a state examination, adding enough points to enable the student to pass the test. The term originated with grading of the New York Regents examinations, where teachers work in groups to evaluate essays written by students in their school.

---

seat time: A measure of the time that students spend in class. The Carnegie unit, for example, is based on how many hours a student spent in the study of a particular subject; a certain number of Carnegie units is usually required by high schools for graduation and by many colleges for admission. Critics of the measure of seat time say that it is meaningless when compared with other ways of gauging student learning and mastery, such as end-of-course examinations, performance assessments, and portfolios of student work.

---

secondary source: A book, article, or other document that contains information summarizing or referring to one or more original, or primary, sources. Contrast **primary source**.

---

secular schools: Schools that are not associated with any religious denomination. Public schools and independent private schools are secular schools, as opposed to religious schools controlled by sectarian groups. Contrast **religious schools**.

---

seed idea: The main idea or theme in a piece of written work produced by a student. This pedagogical concept is part of the writing process and of the writing workshop model. "Nurturing the seed idea" means writing more about the main theme, adding details and possibly dialogue. Part of this process involves "zooming in" on the main idea and perhaps "changing the lens" to make the idea clearer. See also **workshop model; writing process**.

self-directed learning: Learning that an individual chooses to undertake and direct on his or her own.

self-discipline: The ability to control one's emotions and to achieve one's goals through persistence and hard work.

self-esteem: Confidence in or satisfaction with oneself. During the 1980s and 1990s, some educators made almost a fetish of self-esteem as the goal of schooling and life. Students engaged in group activities that were intended to reinforce their self-love by chanting slogans like "I am somebody, I love myself." Social scientists who examined the concept pointed out that self-love is narcissism, that self-assertion is often no more than boasting, and that these traits and behaviors are not necessarily healthy for individuals or for society. Roy Baumeister of Case Western Reserve University drew together research showing that bullies were known for their high self-esteem, which was easily wounded because it was not built on anything solid. Better than self-esteem, research and common sense suggest, are self-discipline, self-respect, and self-reliance. These are traits that lead to the dogged pursuit of goals rather than to self-satisfaction.

self-monitoring: The act of paying attention to one's own work to make sure that it is clear and makes sense. During reading, self-monitoring students attend to meaning and use such fix-up strategies as rereading and reading ahead to clarify meaning; during writing, they reflect on the clarity of the message and on the features of text (words, grammar, and conventions) that are necessary to communicate effectively with an audience. During shared and guided reading, students self-monitor by thinking aloud to share their understanding of a text with the teacher or with other students. Critics complain that *self-monitoring* is jargon for a commonsense practice. See also **metacognition**.

seniority: A statutory system for protecting the job security of employees with the longest periods of service in a district or county office of education. With few exceptions, the seniority list is used to determine which employees will be the first to be laid off or to be rehired. Critics of the seniority system believe that performance should count more than longevity.

sentence combining: A strategy that teaches students to write more complex sentences.

separation of church and state: The belief that religion and government should act independently of each other. Based on interpretation of the First Amendment of the U.S. Constitution and reinforced in numerous rulings of the U.S. Supreme Court, government programs may not advance religion. Because the language of the First Amendment is broad and because there are conflicting decisions, opponents of this concept insist that the supposed "wall of separation" between church and state is not very high or solid.

service learning: Community service by students in a nonschool setting. Service learning aims to deepen students' learning and promote problem solving by having them engage in socially useful activities in the local community. Service learning is sometimes voluntary and sometimes required for high school graduation.

***Sesame Street*:** A program for preschool children on public television that aims to teach basic literacy skills, healthy habits, and social skills, conveying these lessons mostly through puppets. Launched in 1969, the program is internationally distributed and has received numerous awards. Critics over the years have complained that the show contributes to children's television addiction and shortened attention spans, but no amount of criticism has lessened the popularity of the program.

sex education: Instruction on human sexual anatomy, intercourse, and reproduction, as well as on how to avoid pregnancy and sexually transmitted diseases.

shared book room: A room in a balanced literacy school containing a collection of books that are "leveled," meaning they are designated for particular grades or reading levels. A shared book room is different from a library, which contains all sorts of books and other resources from which students may choose, regardless of their grade level. See also **leveled library; leveled readers**.

---

shared decision making (SDM): A process that involves at least teachers and administrators—but sometimes also support staff, students, parents, and members of the local community—in making decisions that affect teaching and learning in their school. As part of this process, a site leadership team compiles a needs assessment and then develops an action plan for school improvement. This action plan is then referred to the larger school community and is discussed, approved, modified, or rejected. The process of improvement through shared decision making is a continuous cycle. See also **school-based decision making (SBDM); site-based decision making (SBDM)**.

---

shared reading: A pedagogical technique that divides students into pairs to read together, taking turns listening and reading. This activity is an aspect of the constructivist method of teaching reading and is usually found in balanced literacy classrooms.

---

shared writing: A pedagogical technique that divides students into pairs to read and discuss each other's writing projects. This activity is usually found in balanced literacy classrooms using the writing process or the writers' workshop model.

---

sheltered English: A form of simplified English that includes hand gestures to help convey meaning. Teachers use it primarily to communicate with limited-English-proficient students.

---

sheltered English immersion: An instructional approach to teaching students with limited English proficiency in which nearly all classroom instruction is conducted in English but with an awareness of the needs of English language learners. Proposition 227, passed by California voters in 1998, mandated one year of sheltered English immersion before students were transferred into regular English language classes.

---

sight words: A limited number of commonly used words that young children are encouraged to memorize as a whole, without decoding them. Advocates of whole-word instruction believe that being able to recognize a large number of sight words will give students a fast start in learning to read. Advocates of phonics, however, believe that students should focus on learning to decode new words.

silent reading: Time devoted in class to reading quietly and individually, without speaking out loud. See also **Sustained Silent Reading (SSR)**. Contrast **oral reading**.

Singapore mathematics: A mathematics program based on the curriculum used in the schools of Singapore. Some school districts and many homeschooling parents choose this program because of Singapore's success in international assessments. The program teaches mathematics in a logical, sequential manner, moving from concrete examples to abstract principles, and expects students to solve math problems in their heads.

single salary schedule: A table for calculating teachers' pay based on their years of experience and graduate coursework. The overwhelming majority of public school districts adhere to such a schedule. Critics contend that those who teach in areas where there are shortages, who teach in specialty fields, or whose work is in greater demand should receive additional pay. Contrast **bonus pay; merit pay**.

single-sex education: Classes or schools that enroll only girls or only boys. Advocates of single-sex schooling claim that it helps adolescent students concentrate on their studies, free of distracting socialization with or of potential intimidation by the opposite sex. Critics claim that single-sex education is comparable to racially segregated schooling.

site-based decision making (SBDM): A school management approach that involves the staff in all important decisions, including those related to curriculum, schedules, staffing, budget, facilities, and resources. See also **school-based decision making (SBDM); shared decision making (SDM)**.

situated learning: A theory holding that learning occurs best as a function of a particular real-life context, culture, or activity, as contrasted with typical classroom learning, which is abstract, inauthentic, and out of context. Situated learning is informal and may result from student activity, collaboration, or social interaction. Critics of situated learning view the theory as an attempt to introduce a method that is incidental, haphazard, and of dubious effectiveness.

sixty-five percent solution: A proposal by a Washington, D.C.–based organization called First Class Education to mandate that 65 percent of school dollars be spent directly on classrooms as a way to cut administrative overhead. Not surprisingly, it is opposed by administrators; teachers; librarians and certain specialists (who are cut out of the movement's definition of classroom expenses); and others, who call it a simplistic response to school finance issues.

skills: Competencies or abilities, mental or physical, that may be improved by practice.

small learning community (SLC): A school or a grouping with a relatively small student body, in the range of 300–500 students. Small learning communities are usually high schools, created in reaction to the mega–high schools that typically contain thousands of students on one campus. A small learning community may be a school within a school or a small, freestanding high school. Advocates believe that small learning communities lead to increased student attendance and motivation, due in part to more intensive interactions with adults in the school. Critics worry that small high schools may eventually lower achievement because they lack the staff to provide advanced courses in mathematics, science, and foreign languages. See also **minischool; school within a school (SWAS)**.

small schools movement: A movement initiated in the 1970s, mainly in New York City, to establish small schools. Some of these schools were alternative schools for adolescents in need of intensive remediation, whereas others set out to demonstrate that students would get a better education in schools containing fewer than 500 students. Interest in the small schools movement was propelled by pioneers Deborah Meier and her Central Park East schools in East Harlem in New York City and Theodore Sizer and his Coalition of Essential Schools. The movement continued to grow during the 1980s and 1990s and gained momentum with the commitment of $1 billion by the Bill and Melinda Gates Foundation in the late 1990s. With funding from the Gates Foundation, many cities across the United States agreed to divide their high schools into small schools. Advocates claim that small schools offer a warmer, more personalized climate than do large schools and consequently boast higher achievement, attendance, and graduation rates. Critics contend that the small schools are unable to mount a strong curriculum with advanced courses and that the administrative costs of small schools are excessive, the burden on teachers is greater, and the academic results are uncertain.

SMART Board: Interactive whiteboard used in classrooms for collaboration and presentations. Although SMART Board is a specific brand, the term is often used generically to refer to any interactive whiteboard.

social capital: The relationships among people, built on shared values, that create a sense of community, a sense of trust, and a willingness to help one another. Sociologists such as James Coleman have found that the social capital of a family or community gives important initial advantages to children before they start school and supports their motivation to learn during their school years.

social content guidelines: The directions for textbook publishers developed by the state of California. These directions tell publishers what information their textbooks must include and exclude with regard to groups identified by race, ethnicity, gender, age, disability, economic status, or other criteria. California not only requires proportional representation of listed groups but also prohibits adverse reflection on them—meaning that any "descriptions, depictions, labels, or rejoinders that tend to demean, stereotype, or patronize" any listed group are prohibited. The guidelines also require proportional representation of entrepreneurs, managers, and labor groups and ban adverse reflection on any particular occupation. In response to California's social content guidelines, publishers are careful to avoid adverse reflection on any group in history textbooks and to eliminate potentially controversial literary selections. See also **adverse reflection; bias and sensitivity review.**

socialization: A process by which people learn to cooperate with others toward common goals, or at least to act appropriately when placed in contact with others.

socializing intelligence: The expectation that students can be taught to think intelligently by developing "habits of mind" to solve problems, not just to stockpile tidbits of knowledge.

social promotion: The policy of promoting students from one grade to the next with their age group even though they have not mastered the skills and knowledge that are considered appropriate for the next grade level. See also **promotion.** Contrast **retention.**

social studies: A broad conglomeration of school studies that includes history, economics, geography, government, civics, and sociology, as well as consumer education, personal decision making, current events, global studies, environmental studies, ethnic studies, gender studies, and other nondisciplinary studies related to contemporary issues and the social sciences.

socioeconomically disadvantaged: A term describing students who participate in the federal free/reduced-price meal program because of low family income.

socioeconomic status: A term used to describe the home backgrounds of individuals or groups, taking into account such elements as family income and education attainment.

Socratic seminar: A class discussion in which the teacher advances a lesson on a specific topic or text by interacting with students, continually asking challenging questions about an assigned reading, and responding to the students' answers by posing more questions. This method, proposed by Mortimer Adler in the Paideia Plan, is intended to encourage students to think rather than just look for the "right" answer. Socratic seminars are based on primary-source works of literature, philosophy, and history instead of textbooks. See also **developmental lesson; Paideia Program.**

special day classes: Full-day classes taught by certified special education teachers outside the general education program for students who have intensive learning disabilities, speech or language impairments, serious emotional disturbances, cognitive delays, or other impairments. A student may eventually be mainstreamed or enter a full inclusion program as appropriate according to his or her Individualized Education Program.

special education: Programs to identify and meet the education needs of students with emotional, learning, or physical disabilities. Federal law requires that all students with disabilities be provided a free and appropriate education according to the specifications of an Individualized Education Program from infancy until 21 years of age. See also **free appropriate public education (FAPE); Individualized Education Program (IEP); Individuals with Disabilities Education Act (IDEA).**

special needs: A term used to describe the needs of students with disabilities that must be addressed by their teachers and their school, as required by federal law.

speech codes: Regulations adopted on many college campuses that prohibit certain kinds of speech deemed offensive by various groups—for example, jokes that make fun of women, blacks, Hispanics, or individuals with disabilities. Advocates of speech codes claim that they are necessary to protect campus civility and to eliminate verbal harassment. Critics claim that they stifle freedom of speech and violate Constitutional protections. In public higher education, speech codes have been largely eliminated by litigation, but many private universities continue to enforce them.

spelling: The act of correctly identifying the combination and sequence of letters that constitute a word. Throughout the 19th century and for most of the 20th century, educators valued accurate spelling. Spelling bees were a popular class and school activity, sometimes performed for the edification and entertainment of the local community. In the 1970s, however, spelling was derided as an unimportant skill that impeded students' ability to write with facility, and teachers were discouraged from teaching spelling or correcting students' inaccurately spelled words. Even now, teachers are often advised in their professional studies that correct student spelling is unimportant. It should be noted, however, that computers demand accurate spelling; even a single wrong letter may direct a computer user to the wrong Web site or produce erroneous information, for example.

spelling inventory: A spelling list.

Sputnik: The world's first space satellite, launched into outer space by the Soviet Union in 1957. This event produced a strong reaction in the United States. Political leaders feared that U.S. schools had failed to prepare a generation of students in science, mathematics, engineering, and foreign languages. Because critics like Arthur Bestor had been saying the same thing for most of that decade, the public schools were blamed for their low standards and diffuse programs. In response to Sputnik, the U.S. Congress passed the National Defense Education Act in 1958, which provided federal funding for science, mathematics, engineering, foreign languages, and other subjects that were considered neglected. This act was a significant expansion of the federal role in education.

staff development days: Days set aside during the school year—usually on school days—when teachers complete professional development or have time to complete work in their classrooms.

stakeholders: Groups that are assumed to have a direct interest in decisions about education—for example, parents, teachers, administrators, taxpayers, employers, and the general public. When a commission is formed to make recommendations about a problem in education, it is customary to include representatives of those groups and others who are presumed to "hold a stake" in the deliberations.

standard: An officially sanctioned description of what a student is expected to learn and how well it should be learned in specific subjects taught in school. Standards may be created by school districts, states, federal agencies, subject-matter organizations, or advocacy groups. Although the federal government is by law barred from creating or influencing curriculum, various federal agencies have done so, including the National Science Foundation and the U.S. Department of Education. Following the example of the National Assessment Governing Board, which supervises the federally funded National Assessment of Educational Progress, most states identify achievement levels on their tests as basic (adequate); proficient (skilled); or advanced (superior). See also **content standards; performance standards**.

---

standard English: The language that is used by the vast majority of newspapers, magazines, and books published in the United States, as well as by most television networks, government agencies, universities, and employers. Critics object that requiring students to learn standard English discriminates against those who do not speak or write standard English and privileges those who do. Yet the ability to read, speak, and comprehend standard English is necessary for anyone who hopes to advance in school, higher education, the professions, or the business world.

---

standardized test: A test designed to be administered and scored in a standard, consistent manner. Standardized tests are in the same format for all takers and often rely on multiple-choice questions. All students take the test under the same conditions, receiving the same instructions and time limits, although accommodations are usually made for students with disabilities. Norm-referenced tests and criterion-referenced tests are types of standardized tests. Such tests are supposed to be valid, reliable, and fair. See also **criterion-referenced test (CRT); fairness; norm-referenced test (NRT); reliability; validity**.

---

standards-based education: An approach to schooling that begins with agreement among educators about what students should learn in each grade level, what level of achievement should be expected, and how academic performance will be evaluated. Standards for content, for performance, and for evaluation should be aligned so that what is taught determines what is tested. Standards-based education aims to improve achievement by establishing clear and challenging benchmarks; to ensure that teachers know what to teach and students know what they are expected to learn; and to make learning expectations fair and accessible, so that all students have the same opportunity to achieve them.

---

standards-based reform: An effort by the federal government, states, and school districts to reach consensus on and establish standards for what students should know and be able to do at each grade or developmental level. This externally mandated strategy aims to improve education by stipulating what students are supposed to learn; testing to see whether they've learned it; and establishing consequences for students, educators, and schools that do not meet the standards. The movement for standards-based reform began in 1983 with the publication of the federal report *A Nation at Risk*, which claimed that the United States was threatened by "a rising tide of mediocrity." In 1989, President George H. W. Bush convened the nation's governors for an education summit to set national goals for U.S. education. In 1991, President Bush launched the America 2000 program and urged communities, school districts, and states to adopt the voluntary national goals established by the initiative. In 1994, the U.S. Congress passed President Bill Clinton's Goals 2000 program, which distributed funds to states to develop their own standards and tests. In 2002, President George W. Bush signed into law the No Child Left Behind Act, which required each state to test every student in grades 3–8 annually, according to the state's own standards and assessments. Two decades after *A Nation at Risk*, every U.S. state had its own standards and tests. Some critics have suggested that this reform is too fragmented and that the United States should adopt national standards, particularly in such crucial areas as mathematics and science. Other critics object to standards-based reform because they oppose a set curriculum and standardized testing as arbitrary impositions on teachers' freedom to teach.

---

standard units of credit: Courses passed by a student.

***Stanford 9* (SAT-9):** A test officially known as the "Stanford Achievement Test Series, Ninth Edition" and published by Harcourt Assessment. It is a standardized, nationally normed, multiple-choice test that measures basic skills in math, reading, and other areas.

state education agency (SEA): The agency primarily responsible for supervising a state's public schools.

state textbook adoption process: The process conducted by nearly half of all U.S. states to review and select the textbooks that school districts are permitted to buy with state funds. In these states, textbook publishers present their books to special committees that are empowered by the state education department or the state board of education to recommend adoption or rejection. These committees hold public hearings at which any individual or organization can speak out for or against a particular textbook. These hearings, and the adoption process as a whole, are frequently the target of organized protests by small groups that object to some portion of a textbook and demand that the state either compel the publisher to revise the textbook or, if the publisher refuses, reject the book. State officials often require publishers to remove "offensive" or "insensitive" words or descriptions, even if the language in the book is factually accurate. For example, a religious or cultural group may not like certain references to its ancestors' practices, or a feminist group may complain that more than half of the names in a textbook refer to men. Textbook adoption decisions made by large states, especially California and Texas, have an especially large financial effect on publishers, which cannot accept the financial risk of refusing to remove controversial material. Critics have suggested that the state textbook adoption process be eliminated because it gives too much power to small vocal pressure groups to impose changes without regard to accuracy or scholarship. See also **bias and sensitivity review; social content guidelines**.

stem: A question or statement on a multiple-choice test that poses a choice for the test taker. See also **distracter; foils; multiple-choice item**.

story map: A graphic used to illustrate the various elements of a short story. Typically, these elements include setting (time and place); conflict; protagonist; antagonist; minor characters; and elements of the plot (exposition, inciting incident, rising action, climax, crisis, falling action, resolution, and denouement).

story seeds: Ideas around which a student might build a story. Every story, for example, involves a conflict, so a teacher could provide a student with a conflict as a story seed and have the student create the setting, the characters, the incident that starts the conflict, and so on.

stovepipe organization: An organization whose different functions are separated so that each department has a narrow, rigid set of responsibilities and there is little discussion or collaboration among the various sectors.

strand: A group of related themes or concepts within an overall curricular area. For example, a social studies curriculum might be divided into such strands as citizenship, history, economics, geography, legal systems, political systems, and so on.

strategy: A plan or tactic to solve a problem or carry out a decision. In education, a strategy refers to almost everything that a teacher or a student does in a classroom—asking a question, reading a story, figuring out the meaning of a word, planning the next day's lesson, and so on.

stretch it out: A replacement for the customary expression "sound it out," referring to a technique for analyzing an unfamiliar word. When a student who has had little exposure to phonetic methods of analyzing letters and words confronts a new word, the literacy coach may tell the student to "stretch it out like a rubber band" in hopes of finding the meaning of the word or perhaps familiar associations.

striving reader: A student whose reading skills are below grade level.

student-centered education: See **child-centered education**.

student study team: A team of educators, convened at the request of a classroom teacher, parent, or counselor, that designs in-class intervention techniques to discuss the needs of a particular student. The team may consist of the primary teacher; the parent or guardian of the student; two specialists (for example, in speech therapy, psychology, or counseling); a teacher who does not teach the student in any class; and the principal. Six weeks after implementing a program for the student, the team reconvenes to determine whether further steps, including a transfer to special education classes, are necessary.

student teacher: A teacher in training in a teacher education program. Student teachers practice teaching under the supervision of regular classroom teachers.

study of models: A teaching technique to hone students' writing abilities that consists of reading, analyzing, and emulating good models of writing.

substitute teacher: A teacher hired to temporarily replace a regular teacher who is absent for a short period of time.

subtractive bilingualism: A description of a bilingual program in which students become proficient in a second language, which then replaces their first language in the curriculum. Contrast **additive bilingualism**.

Success for All (SFA): A program that combines cooperative group learning and individualized instruction to teach reading, writing, and mathematics to students in elementary and middle schools. Developed by Robert Slavin at Johns Hopkins University, SFA has shown particular efficacy with students who come from disadvantaged and poor communities. Although it is deemed effective in independent studies, critics dislike it because it is scripted and thus limits the teacher's creativity.

Suggestopedia: A method of foreign-language instruction developed by Bulgarian psychologist Georgi Lozanov in the 1970s that uses the power of positive suggestion. Teachers trained in Suggestopedia's techniques create a calm physical classroom environment that relaxes the students and lowers their affective filter, or resistance to learning. The teacher first introduces the words and grammar of the lesson. Then, during a concert session, students listen to the teacher read the lesson while Baroque music plays in the background. Other forms of art, such as poetry, drama, and puppetry, are also employed to stimulate students' perceptions. The students sing songs and play games, using what they have learned, and then interact with one another in the new language, without correction. The method is also referred to as *desuggestopedia* to reflect advances in its theoretical development.

suitcase college: A nonresidential institution of higher education; a commuter campus. This term also refers to a residential college that many students happen to leave for the weekend, generally because their homes are nearby.

summarization: The process of determining important information in a text and explaining it briefly in one's own words.

summative assessment: An assessment used to document students' achievement at the end of a unit or course or an evaluation of the end product of a student's learning activity. Final exams are an example of summative assessment. See also **formative assessment**.

summative evaluation: Evaluation carried out for the purpose of gathering information to assess the overall worth of educational staff, programs, and products. Evaluation is often motivated by a prospective decision, such as purchasing a product, adopting a program, or determining the amount of a raise for staff. See also **formative evaluation**.

Summerhill: A private English boarding school founded in 1921 by A. S. Neill to implement his belief in the value of eliminating all compulsion from children's lives. The school was initially opened under a different name in Germany in 1921; in 1923, the school moved to a house called Summerhill in Lyme Regis in the south of England, where it enrolled five pupils. Enrollment was never more than a few dozen students, but the school gained an international reputation because of its radical belief in children's freedom and Neill's widely read publications. His book *Summerhill* was a best seller in the United States in the 1960s and became required reading in hundreds of universities. Neill was a spokesman for the most permissive wing of the progressive education movement, proposing that children should be free to decide how to live, what to learn, and whether they wanted to learn. Neill believed that "the function of the child is to live his own life—not the life that his anxious parents think he should live, nor a life according to the purpose of the educator who thinks he knows best."

supplemental educational services: Additional learning opportunities that school districts are required to provide under the No Child Left Behind Act to low-income students who attend schools that have failed to make adequate yearly progress for three years in a row. Parents may select the appropriate services for their child from a list of approved providers (which sometimes includes the district teachers), and the school district pays for the services with federal funds. Supplemental educational services must be provided outside the regular school day and must be high-quality, research-based, and specifically designed to increase academic achievement.

support staff: Secretaries and others who assist school administrators.

suspension: The removal of a student from classes or from school because of unacceptable behavior. Suspension is temporary and may last from one day to several days, depending on school rules.

Sustained Silent Reading (SSR): A time set aside in the school day for uninterrupted, independent reading. Homework and conversation are not allowed during SSR periods. Variations on SSR include Free Voluntary Reading (FVR); Uninterrupted Sustained Silent Reading (USSR); Positive Outcomes While Enjoying Reading (POWER); Daily Individual Reading Time (DIRT); Sustained Quiet Uninterrupted Reading Time (SQUIRT); and Drop Everything and Read (DEAR). See also **silent reading**. Contrast **oral reading**.

syllabus: A summary outline of a program of study that explains in detail what teachers will teach, what students are expected to learn, and what the examination for the course will cover.

systematic instruction: A teaching approach that identifies the specific steps needed to teach a given lesson. Systematic instruction includes clear objectives describing the content to be learned, detailed strategies to teach that content, and diagnostic assessments to determine whether students have mastered the content. See also **Direct Instruction (DI)**.

systematic phonics: Direct reading instruction that explicitly teaches the relationships between letters and sounds in a sequence of interconnected lessons.

systemic school reform: A plan to implement changes simultaneously in all aspects of the school system—including standards, curriculum, instruction, assessment, and staff training—to ensure that all parts are aligned around a common reform strategy.

Talented Tenth: An expression referring to the most gifted students of any particular group. The phrase was coined in 1903 by W. E. B. DuBois, a prominent African American scholar, to describe the gifted black students who would provide leadership for the future. He wrote, "The Talented Tenth of the Negro race must be made leaders of thought and missionaries of culture among their people. No others can do this work and Negro colleges must train men for it. The Negro race, like all other races, is going to be saved by its exceptional men."

targeted assistance program (TAP): A program operating at schools that receive Title I, Part A, funding but are ineligible or have chosen not to operate a schoolwide program under Title I. Using Title I money, TAPs provide services only to eligible students identified as having the greatest educational need. School staff members determine which services and activities will be provided to which students. Non–Title I students are not eligible to receive Title I services in a TAP school. See also **pullout program; schoolwide program; Title I**.

task-based instruction: An instructional approach that relies on specific activities to teach students the skills and knowledge they need in the "real world." The curriculum designer or teacher identifies specific needs—such as taking part in a job interview, applying for a credit card, ordering from a menu, or finding one's way in an unfamiliar city—and builds the daily activities of the classroom around these tasks. See also **scientific management; Taylorism**.

task-oriented learning: A learning approach in which students are expected to complete specific assigned jobs, or tasks, to gain mastery. Advocates of task-oriented instruction laud it because it is experiential and hands-on, as opposed to instruction that relies on books and lectures.

tax credits: A program offered by several U.S. states that allows parents to take a deduction on their state income taxes for approved educational expenses, such as books, uniforms, supplies, computers, tutors, and, in some cases, tuition and transportation. The purpose of tax credits is to extend financial help to families that send their children to nonpublic schools, but to meet constitutional tests, the tax credit must be made available to all families (or at least to those that meet certain income restrictions).

Taylorism: Attitudes or practices based on the time and motion studies by Frederick Taylor, a social engineer of the early 20th century who sought to make factory workers more efficient and productive by studying their ways of working. The implication of the term is that management cares only for efficiency and not for the quality of the work produced by teachers or students or for the educational values imparted. See also **scientific management; task-based instruction**.

teachable moment: A confluence of experience and instruction that suddenly awakens student interest and gives life to what is taught. A teachable moment may occur as the result of a current event, of a school or classroom occurrence, or of something that happened to a student or teacher. Suddenly, a concept that once seemed abstract becomes clear and important. Teachable moments may also occur between parents and children, as parents teach spontaneous everyday lessons about behavior, morals, ethics, and values.

teacher-centered instruction: A pedagogical approach in which the teacher decides what and how to teach. See also **teacher-**

directed classroom. Contrast **child-centered education; learner-centered classroom**.

---

teacher certification: The teaching license issued by states to teachers who have completed a program at a state-approved institution of higher education; taken the required courses in pedagogy (and sometimes subject matter); and fulfilled other requirements, including practice teaching. In most states, teachers who have not received state certification are not permitted to teach in public schools and will be issued only an emergency license. Because of a shortage of qualified teachers, however, many states have developed alternative certification programs to admit people into the teaching profession who have not taken the specified courses in pedagogy or met other requirements. See also **alternative certification; certified employees**.

---

teacher-directed classroom: A classroom in which the teacher is in charge and makes all the important decisions about the content and pace of instruction; also known as the *teacher-dominated classroom*. The *teacher-directed classroom* is sometimes used as a derogatory term compared unfavorably with the *learner-centered classroom*, where students are in charge of their own learning. See also **teacher-centered instruction**. Contrast **child-centered education; learner-centered classroom**.

---

teacher empowerment: An administrative decision to grant to teachers a large degree of autonomy with regard to their schedules, the instructional program, and the curricula in their classrooms.

---

teacher-proof curriculum: A curriculum that is presumably so well designed and so carefully scripted that it cannot be ruined by a mediocre teacher. Some curriculum designers have pinned their hopes on computer-programmed instruction as a possible teacher-proof curriculum that cannot be distorted even by poor teaching. Understandably, teachers find such curricula to be offensive and condescending. See also **programmed learning**.

---

teachers' assistants: Paid aides or volunteers who assist teachers in the classroom. Teachers' assistants may tutor students or provide clerical assistance to the teacher.

teachers colleges: Colleges first created in the early to mid–19th century as *normal schools*, specifically for the purposes of training teachers and establishing teaching standards. These normal schools were formed alongside *common schools* as part of the larger movement toward universal education. The original idea of normal schools is sometimes confused with the current concept of schools of education, but the two models are rooted in different conceptions of curriculum and professionalism. Curriculum in the normal schools integrated subject-matter methods and pedagogical methods. When schools of education were created in the early years of the 20th century, they were typically dominated by behavioral psychologists who assumed that it was possible to separate subject-matter methods and pedagogical methods. During the late 19th and early 20th centuries, all normal schools either closed because of low enrollments or were transformed into regional state universities that now consider teacher education as only one minor part of the institutions' larger academic and professional reasons for existence.

Teach For America (TFA): An organization that recruits college graduates to teach for two years in low-income public schools. TFA was founded in 1989 by Wendy Kopp, who proposed the idea in her senior thesis at Princeton University and then raised money to start the organization. Teachers in TFA participate in a summer preparation institute before starting to teach. Because members of TFA can enter teaching without taking courses at a school of education, TFA is an alternate route into the teaching profession. However, because TFA teachers must meet state requirements, they take education courses while teaching.

teaching for understanding: A pedagogical method that focuses on teaching students to understand new concepts rather than memorize discrete facts. Although this term has been used to refer specifically to deep, meaningful learning, it's really the goal of all instruction: all teachers want their students to understand, not just recall and recite, whatever was taught.

teaching to the test: The practice of devoting extra time and attention in the classroom to the skills and knowledge that will be assessed on the district or state test. Critics claim that it reduces education to a limited range of skills, ignores the importance of comprehension, and neglects subjects that are not tested, such as history, civics, geography, and the arts.

teach the child, not the subject: The quintessential slogan of the progressive, child-centered movement of the 20th century. It is certainly true that the health and welfare of the child are more important than academic subject matter. However, the slogan sets up an unfortunate and unnecessary dichotomy between the child's social, physical, and emotional well-being and the teacher's responsibility to teach the child the knowledge and skills that are essential elements of a good education. Both are important. See also **child-centered education; meeting the needs of the whole child**.

team teaching: An instructional method in which two or more teachers collaboratively teach a group of students. Teaching teams may teach one subject to multiple classes or teach all the core subjects to a single cluster of students for the school year. In the former arrangement, teachers may take turns instructing the entire group or divide the class into smaller sections that rotate between the teachers. In the latter arrangement, teachers meet frequently to plan curriculum and address student strengths and weaknesses.

tech prep: A four-year program (the last two years of high school plus two years of community college) that leads to an associate degree or a two-year certificate in a specific career field. The carefully integrated and sequenced curriculum includes a common core of mathematics, science, communications, and technologies. Tech prep provides training for the average student who does not want to attend a four-year college but wants to prepare for a career.

tenure: A legal guarantee that a teacher cannot be removed from his or her position without cause and that any removal will be done in accordance with due process. Teachers in public schools usually gain tenure if they have served satisfactorily for three to five years. Tenure was created to protect teachers from capricious administrators and to preserve their academic freedom.

Terman, Lewis (1877–1956): A psychologist at Stanford University and a pioneer in the development and popularization of intelligence tests. Holding that intelligence was innate, fixed, and inherited, Terman strongly believed that intelligence tests could quickly determine, as early as age 6, not only how smart a student was but also his or her likely educational attainment and career prospects. Terman was also an important figure in drawing attention to education for the gifted. See also **intelligence quotient (IQ)**.

test: A series of questions intended to determine whether and how well students have learned certain skills and knowledge. A test may be developed by a teacher or by test publishers for the school district, the state, or the federal government. If developed by a teacher, a test is supposed to cover what was taught in his or her classroom. If developed by a test publishing company for a government unit, it is usually standardized and permits comparison among students in different schools, even across different jurisdictions. See also **assessment**.

test modifications: Changes in testing conditions made in response to the needs of the student taking the test, especially a student with disabilities or a student who is not proficient in the English language. See also **accommodations**.

test prep: Time spent in class learning how to take a test and practicing the kinds of questions that appear on tests (e.g., multiple-choice questions and essay questions). Although students do need to become familiar with the format of the test they will take, an inordinate amount of classroom time devoted to test prep may mean less time devoted to instruction in science, literature, history, mathematics, and other studies. Taken to an extreme, test prep may boost scores on tests in the short run, especially in the early grades, while undermining the quality of education.

text-based reading: Reading from something that is in print, such as a book.

textbook: The basic instructional tool for most subjects taught in U.S. schools. In the absence of a state or national curriculum, the textbook is the main vehicle to convey the content of each course. It is usually very heavy because it is loaded with graphics and other visual distractions from the subject, and its contents are written in short, choppy sentences on the assumption that they make the book easier to read. Publishers produce textbooks with these characteristics because they are trying to please text-book adoption committees in states that have huge buying power (mainly California and Texas). These committees are apparently impressed by lively graphics, regardless of the books' effective-ness as teaching tools.

text-to-self connection: A learning strategy applied by elemen-tary students while reading a text. Prompted by the teacher, stu-dents ask themselves whether the text they are reading reminds them of something that happened in their own lives. Advocates claim that making these connections helps students think about and understand what they are learning. Critics contend that the approach is artificial, makes reading a technical process, and does not help students appreciate literature that does not relate to their own lives.

text-to-text connection: The act of comparing one reading pas-sage with another.

thematic initiative: A program that is organized around a com-mon idea or theme.

thematic unit: A unit of study whose lessons are focused on a specific theme, sometimes covering a variety of subject areas. For example, the theme of inequality may be explored by study-ing the caste system in India and slavery in the American South. These units may be used as an alternative approach to teaching history, but history educators are critical of the tendency to teach such content without regard to a chronological framework. Themes that lack historical context, the critics say, are superficial and confusing.

theme schools: Schools that emphasize a particular set of activi-ties or ideas that they think will appeal to students. For example, some schools are dedicated to technology, whereas others focus on the performing arts or on specific vocations. As the movement for small schools accelerated in the 1990s and the early 21st century, there was a large increase in the number of theme high schools, some with esoteric or highly specialized themes (e.g., the sports professions or world architecture). See also **Bill and Melinda Gates Foundation**.

theory theory: The idea that very young children actively construct and test theories about how the world works. According to this concept, a child holds an established theory until he or she encounters an anomaly that forces a paradigm shift and the adoption of a new theory. Theory theory is an application of ideas first expressed by Thomas Kuhn in 1962 in *The Structure of Scientific Revolutions*. See also **paradigm**.

think-aloud strategy: The process of talking explicitly about what one is reading. The think-aloud process, which involves questioning, accessing prior knowledge, and making predictions, helps students recognize the strategies they are using to understand a text.

Thorndike, Edward Lee (1874–1949): A founder of the field of educational psychology. Thorndike, who began his work with studies of animal behavior, spent most of his career at Teachers College, Columbia University, where he sought to make the study of education more scientific and was a leading figure in the progressive education movement. As a behaviorist, he promulgated various "laws of learning" based on connections between stimulus and response studies. He opposed such allegedly useless studies as Latin and Greek and any other subjects that supposedly "trained the mind" in favor of studies that were relevant to students' interests and needs. Thorndike was a pioneer in the development of standardized tests and intelligence tests and, like most other educational psychologists, believed that intelligence was measurable, hereditary, and immutable.

threshold hypothesis: The belief among advocates of bilingual education that individuals with high levels of proficiency in two languages experience cognitive advantages in language skills and intellectual growth over those with low levels of proficiency in two languages, who have significant cognitive deficits.

time on task: The number of minutes during an hour and the number of hours during a day that students spend actively engaged in learning in the classroom, as opposed to the amount of time spent changing classes, chatting, or engaging in other nonlearning situations.

Tinker v. Des Moines Independent Community School District: A decision by the U.S. Supreme Court in 1969 that defined First Amendment rights for students. In this case, local school officials banned the wearing of black armbands by students who were protesting the war in Vietnam. The Court's decision held that the students' actions represented symbolic speech protected under the U.S. Constitution. Justice Hugo Black, usually a strong supporter of First Amendment rights, dissented from the 7–2 decision: ". . . If the time has come when pupils . . . can defy and flout orders of school officials to keep their minds on their own schoolwork, it is the beginning of a new revolutionary era of permissiveness in this country fostered by the judiciary."

Title I: A federally funded program designed to improve the academic achievement of low-income students. Title I was first passed in 1965 as part of the Elementary and Secondary Education Act to provide funds for educationally disadvantaged students. Funding is intended to supplement, not replace, state and district funds and is based on the number of low-income students in a school (generally those who are eligible for the free/reduced-price meals program). Title I funds are distributed to school districts, which make allocations to eligible schools according to criteria in the federal law. Schools receiving Title I monies are supposed to involve parents in deciding how those funds are spent and in reviewing progress. See also **Elementary and Secondary Education Act (ESEA); No Child Left Behind Act (NCLB); pullout program; schoolwide program; targeted assistance program (TAP)**.

Title II: A section of the No Child Left Behind Act that provides funding to prepare, train, and recruit high-quality teachers and principals. It also includes grants to integrate technology into the classroom.

Title III: A section of the No Child Left Behind Act that provides funding for language instruction for limited-English-proficient and immigrant students. This funding, which comes on top of any

Title I funding a school might receive, includes specific assessment and parent notification requirements.

Title IX: Federal legislation passed in 1972 that prohibits discrimination by educational institutions on the basis of gender. This law had a dramatic effect on the participation of women in sports, stating that no one could be excluded, on the basis of sex, from participating in any program receiving federal financial assistance. Since all public institutions receive some form of federal assistance, as well as almost every private institution (through federal aid for student tuition), Title IX was understood to cover virtually all educational institutions, both public and private. After some institutions and courts interpreted the law to mean that an equal amount must be spent on both sexes, many colleges created athletics programs for women and curtailed some for men. In 2006, the U.S. Department of Education declared that Title IX did not prohibit single-sex public schools.

top-down reform: Efforts to impose school reform from "the top" by mandates from the federal government, the state legislature, the state department of education, the school board, or the mayor's office. Contrast **bottom-up reform**.

Total Physical Response (TPR): A language-teaching method based on the belief that students will learn better when full bodily motion is involved in the process. Developed by educator and researcher James J. Asher, TPR is supposed to replace the traditional learning strategy of sitting at a desk and reading a book. Verbal commands are replaced by physical ones. For example, teachers may teach the alphabet by having students lie on the floor to form letter shapes or have students learn punctuation by mimicking the shape of a period, a comma, or an exclamation mark. There is some historical precedent for TPR: in the early 19th century, some pedagogues believed that students would learn the alphabet if they ate biscuits baked in the shape of letters, an ineffective practice that eventually disappeared.

touchstone text: A book or an article that serves as a model for writing assignments.

tough love: A regimen that simultaneously involves strict discipline and expressions of caring.

tracking: A common instructional practice that assigns students to courses or curriculum programs with others who have similar academic goals or skills. Tracking often occurs as a result of student self-selection into programs or courses of varying levels of difficulty. In the past, tracking referred to the two separate paths that students chose to follow: college or a vocation. Currently, however, the term *tracking* is used almost interchangeably with the term *ability grouping* and applies to all grade levels. As currently used, it refers to a decision by the school to place students in different classes according to their ability levels, the rationale being that it enables teachers to provide the same level of instruction to each group. This practice is criticized, however, by those who fear that students in low-level ability groups (or tracks) never gain access to challenging instruction. See also **ability grouping; homogeneous grouping**. Contrast **detracking; heterogeneous grouping**.

transcript: A student's secondary school record, which identifies courses taken, grades, graduation status, and attendance. In addition, it often includes scores for such assessments as the Preliminary SAT, the SAT, the ACT, the Iowa Tests of Basic Skills, and advanced placement tests.

transfer of training: The belief that what is learned in one subject or course of study will "transfer," or be applicable in another subject, or even in daily life. For example, habits learned in school, such as concentration, neatness, and prompt completion of assignments, might be transferred to the workplace. Educationists argued about transfer of training in the early decades of the 20th century. Defenders of such subjects as Latin and algebra claimed that they taught clear thinking, which carried over into other studies and became a foundation for life. Progressive critics of the traditional academic curriculum, on the other hand, cited studies by psychologist Edward L. Thorndike allegedly showing that transfer of training was a myth—that "you learn what you learn" and that Latin teaches only Latin, not good judgment or clear thinking. Subsequent studies, however, have demonstrated that certain habits and skills learned in school do transfer across studies and into real-world activities.

transitional bilingual education: A teaching approach in which non-English-speaking students are instructed in two languages—English and their native language—with the goal of helping the students move into the regular English language curriculum in a year or two. As students gain proficiency in English, instruction in their native language decreases, until they have successfully made the transition into the regular curriculum. See also **bilingual education; immersion**.

transitional reader: A student who has moved beyond the beginning stages of learning to read but needs additional support to become a fully independent reader.

transparency: Openness. Transparency means making information about public schools and education clear, user-friendly, and readily accessible to diverse audiences and constituencies, including parents. Whoever seeks information about the cost, performance, or policies of a school or school system (not including personal information about individuals) should be able to get it without difficulty, in a form that enables the user to easily compare one school, system, or state with the next. Measurement and information systems should provide full transparency throughout the public education system. The burden for establishing transparency rests on individual schools, where information is first generated; on district school systems that collect information from the schools; and on states, which accumulate information about schools and districts.

trenches: The front line of education; inside the classroom, where teachers work. Many experienced teachers believe that people who are not "in the trenches" are mere commentators who don't really understand what teachers have to deal with every day.

Trends in International Mathematics and Science Study (TIMSS): A series of international studies and assessments that collect data on the mathematics and science achievement of students from the United States and other countries. So far, TIMSS data have been collected in 1995, 1999, 2003, and 2007.

truant: A student who fails to show up for school without a valid reason. Many cities and school districts have policies to reduce truancy—for example, requiring truants to perform community service, withdrawing their driving privileges, fining their parents, reducing their families' welfare payments, and subjecting their parents to civil fines or even criminal prosecution.

tuition: Payment for instruction. Tuition fees are typically charged by private schools, tutors, and institutions of higher education.

tuning protocol: A process for reflecting on and discussing student work, designed by the Coalition of Essential Schools. First, the facilitator introduces the agenda and the protocol norms and goals, and the participants introduce themselves. Then the teacher takes about 20 minutes to present examples of student work. Next, the group asks clarifying questions, and the facilitator decides whether the questions are *warm* (supportive) or *cool* (distancing). There is a pause for reflection and then a period for feedback, both warm and cool, during which participants respond to the teacher presentation while the teacher remains silent. The teacher then takes at least 15 minutes to reflect on and respond to the questions while the participants remain silent. Finally, the group debriefs by reflecting on the discussion and the protocol. There is also a *California protocol*, a variation of the tuning protocol, in which a school's "analysis team" examines student work and the restructuring of the school in the presence of a group of reflectors.

turn and talk strategy: In a balanced literacy classroom, the practice of getting students to discuss with one another what they have read in their read-aloud group.

turnaround specialists: Individuals, usually veteran school principals, who have been trained to take over a low-performing school and improve student achievement. The term may also refer to businesses that attempt to manage school districts on the basis of their experience in corporate restructuring.

Understanding by Design: A form of curriculum planning that begins with a decision about what students need to learn as the end result. Then the teacher engages in *backward design*, choosing activities that will bring students to the preselected goal. Although the belief that classroom activities should be based on a set curriculum or on set learning goals is not new, this widely used program is attributed to Grant Wiggins and Jay McTighe. See also **backward mapping**.

validity: The extent to which a test does in fact measure or predict what it sets out to measure or predict, as well as the extent to which the inferences people make on the basis of test scores are appropriate and justifiable. Tests can have content validity, criterion validity, construct validity, consequential validity, and face validity. A test that measures what it claims to measure has *content validity*. A test that predicts something that test administrators are interested in predicting has *criterion validity* (also called *predictive validity*). For example, the SAT is meant to predict freshman grades in college. A test that measures psychological constructs (such as intelligence, anxiety, or self-esteem) that it claims to measure has *construct validity. Consequential validity* refers to the consequences of a test or to inferences drawn from the test. For example, the consequence of a number of students failing a test may be that teachers change the curriculum. A test that appears appropriate or relevant to the test taker as well as to teachers and administrators has *face validity*. If a test does not have face validity, the validity of the test as a whole is compromised. See also **fairness; reliability**.

value-added system of accountability: A method of gauging the effect of a school, a teacher, or a program on student learning by measuring and comparing the gains in student test performance over time—for example, comparing a student's current test scores with his or her scores from the previous year. The difference between the two measures represents the learning gain—the "value added" by the school, teacher, or program.

values clarification: A philosophy popularized in the 1970s holding that students should think through difficult moral and ethical dilemmas and make their own choices. This idea spawned numerous programs in the schools, where students made choices about what to do in difficult personal situations, such as whether to engage in premarital sex or take illegal drugs. According to proponents, such programs taught students the process of moral deliberation. However, critics complained that values clarification was relativistic and that the schools were abandoning their moral responsibility in allowing students to make unwise and dangerous decisions.

virtual schools: Internet-based schools that provide online classes. Students can get their lessons on a computer at home or in any other location. Also called *cyber education* and *distance learning*, although the latter term may refer to online classes received by students in a traditional school building. See also **distance learning (DL)**.

visioning: The process of developing a clear idea of what one is trying to accomplish.

vocabulary: The words that students have learned or need to learn to increase their general literacy and their store of knowledge. In general, the greater the students' vocabulary, the greater their capacity to learn new information and new ideas.

vocational education: A program or course of study to prepare students for a specific job, such as repairing automobiles or performing secretarial duties.

vouchers: Payment by the state to underwrite all or part of a student's education expenses at a nonpublic school—whether independent or religious—chosen by the student or the student's family. The theory behind vouchers, as originally espoused by economist Milton Friedman, is that government monopoly of services leads to lessened quality and that competition for good schools would improve all schools by forcing bad ones to close. Friedman advocated *universal vouchers*, a system that would give all parents control over where to send their children to school. In effect, the proposal for universal vouchers would separate the government financing of education from the government operation of all public schools. Some proponents advocate *means-tested vouchers*, which would be allotted only to low-income students. In the early 21st century, the school districts of Milwaukee, Wisconsin, and Cleveland, Ohio, were the only ones that were authorized by their respective state legislatures to offer vouchers to low-income students. In 1998, the U.S. Supreme Court turned down a legal challenge to Milwaukee's program. Cleveland's plan was approved by the U.S. Supreme Court in 2002 (*Zelman v. Simmons-Harris*). The state of Florida enacted a plan to offer vouchers to students in persistently failing schools, but a state court ruled that program unconstitutional in 2005. Vouchers have proven to be extremely controversial and are opposed by teachers' unions and others who fear that they might weaken the public schools. See also **choice**.

walk-through: An organized visit to a classroom or a school to observe teachers and students. Some walk-throughs are collegial, as when teachers observe other teachers or when principals observe other principals. Most, however, are supervisory, as when principals and other administrators visit classrooms to evaluate the quality of teachers' work. At the conclusion of the walk-through, those who have been observed receive feedback and learn how they can improve. The walk-through team is supposed to create documentation for feedback and follow-up sessions. Variants of the walk-through include the *focused walk through* and the *instructionally focused walk-through*.

weighted student funding: A proposal to change the allocation of funding to public schools so that the total amount received by each school would be based not on its staffing, programs, or number of students, but on the needs of its students. The formula would shift funding to schools that have disproportionately large numbers of students with greater needs—for example, those who come from low-income families, who have disabilities, or who are English language learners—and would also increase the funds available to charter schools. Critics of weighted student funding object that it would destabilize successful schools by penalizing those that have large numbers of experienced teachers.

What Works Clearinghouse: A program established in 2002 by the U.S. Department of Education's Institute of Education Sciences to determine which educational interventions are most effective. Its goal is to supply reliable evidence to the public about programs, products, practices, and policies that have demonstrated their effectiveness.

white flight: Exodus from urban neighborhoods and schools by white families, for a variety of reasons. When white flight occurs, as it did in many U.S. cities during the last third of the 20th century, the proportion of minority students in urban schools grows. In some cases, white flight resulted from court orders requiring extensive busing of students to promote racial integration: many white families were unwilling to send their children to schools in unfamiliar neighborhoods. In other cases, white flight occurred as part of a demographic shift of middle-class families (white and black) from the cities to the suburbs. Whatever the reason, the decline in the number and proportion of white students makes racial integration in urban schools difficult: as of 2000, the pupils in most urban districts were predominantly African American and Hispanic.

whole-class instruction: Instruction of the entire class as one group learning the same lesson. In traditional classrooms, teachers alternate whole-class instruction with small-group activities. In progressive or constructivist classrooms, whole-class instruction is minimized or avoided in favor of cooperative group work and individualized instruction.

whole language: A philosophy and teaching method that focuses on reading for meaning in context. In its purest form, as described by one of its major founders, Kenneth Goodman of the University of Arizona, whole language avoids linguistic analysis of any kind, such as phonics instruction, and instead stresses the importance of the wholeness of words and text. In the 1980s, whole language was widely adopted by schools and state education departments across the United States. Whole-language methods fell out of favor, however, in the mid-1990s because of negative results, especially in

California. Its advocates then embraced a similar approach that included attention to phonics instruction, called *balanced literacy*. See also **alphabet; balanced literacy**.

whole math: A derogatory term for mathematics instruction that emphasizes group discussion, essay writing, calculator use in the early grades, and estimating. Critics of whole math claim that this approach ignores basic skills. See also **fuzzy math; Mathematically Correct; math wars; new math; new new math**.

whole-school reform: A reform that seeks to improve school performance by simultaneously aligning all aspects of a school's environment and program with a central guiding vision, theory, or design. Whole-school reform is normally contrasted with the tendency of many schools to adopt multiple unrelated programs. Examples of whole-school reform include such programs as Roots and Wings, Co-nect, America's Choice, Modern Red School-House, Core Knowledge, Expeditionary Learning Schools Outward Bound, Accelerated Schools Project, and other packaged programs that affect all students in a school, not just a subset.

whole-word method: A method for teaching reading that instructs students to look at the whole word and try to recognize it by its shape, familiarity, and context clues, rather than sounding it out phonetically. See also **look-say method**.

word attack skills: A set of strategies used to recognize and pronounce unfamiliar printed words.

word wall: A list of words posted in the classroom on a poster or a wall chart. The list consists of words that are relevant to the lesson being taught and is intended to help students recognize common words, see how they should be spelled, and build vocabulary. In balanced literacy classes, teachers may encourage students to cheer, chant, clap their hands, and engage in other physical responses as new words are added to the word wall.

word web: A graphic organizer used to show loosely associated relations among ideas. To create a word web, follow this procedure: write a word or a phrase in the middle of a piece of paper and circle it. Around the circle, write other words or phrases that come to mind when you think about the first word or phrase. Circle these and draw lines to connect them to the inner circle. Repeat this process with each of the outer circled words and phrases. Continue in this manner until your paper is full.

word work: A term used in balanced literacy classrooms to describe a block of time devoted to teaching phonemic awareness, phonics, fluency, vocabulary, and comprehension.

workshop model: A technique for reading and writing instruction developed by Lucy Calkins of Teachers College, Columbia University. As a rule, the workshop model is constructivist in that there is no curriculum content; yet at the same time, it is prescriptive in describing what teachers and students should do during the time allocated for teaching reading or writing. See also **writing process**.

writing across the curriculum: An expression referring to the belief that writing should be taught as part of every subject in the curriculum. So, for example, the history teacher, the science teacher, and even the math teacher are expected to give writing assignments and to help students become better at expressing themselves in writing.

writing process: A specific sequence of writing activities, including prewriting, drafting, revising, proofreading, and publishing. The writing process was developed as an elementary-level classroom activity intended to put the student's own writing and reflection at the heart of the classroom (as opposed to content that comes from the teacher or from books), but is now found in classes at all levels of education, including universities. See also **workshop model**.

writing strategies: Techniques that help students plan, write, edit, and revise their compositions.

writing through inquiry activities: Activities that involve students in analyzing immediate data so that they develop ideas and content for a writing task.

year-round schooling: A modified school calendar that gives students short breaks throughout the year instead of a traditional three-month summer break. Year-round calendars vary, sometimes within the same school district. Some schools use the staggered schedule to relieve overcrowding; others use it because they believe that the three-month break causes students to forget much of what they learned the previous year. Some schools are on a single-track schedule, in which all students are on vacation at the same time, whereas others operate according to a multitrack schedule, which allows students to take their vacations at different times during the year. Advocates of year-round schooling claim that it saves money, maximizes use of facilities, reduces vandalism, improves student retention of academic content, and reduces dropout rates. Critics contend that the intensive use of school facilities creates maintenance problems and extra expenses (e.g., air-conditioning in the summer); that multitrack schedules cause difficulties for family vacation schedules; and that scheduling extracurricular activities is complicated when team members attend school in different cycles.

zone of proximal development: A term coined by Russian education theorist Lev Vygotsky and popularized in the United States by Jerome Bruner referring to the zone between a student's actual developmental level and his or her level of potential development under adult guidance or in collaboration with more capable peers. The zone of proximal development is where real learning takes place.

Acronyms and Abbreviations

AAC: achievement/ability comparison

AACTE: American Association of Colleges for Teacher Education

AASA: American Association of School Administrators

ABC program: A Better Chance program

ABCTE: American Board for Certification of Teacher Excellence

ABE: Adult Basic Education

ACE: American Council on Education

ACT: A set of college admissions tests and the organization that makes them

ACTAAP: Arkansas Comprehensive Testing, Assessment and Accountability Program

ADA: Americans with Disabilities Act; average daily attendance

ADD: attention deficit disorder

AD/HD: attention deficit hyperactivity disorder

AERA: American Educational Research Association

AFSCME: American Federation of State, County and Municipal Employees

AFT: American Federation of Teachers

AIMS: Arizona's Instrument to Measure Standards

AIR: American Institutes for Research

ALA: American Library Association

AMO: annual measurable objective

AP: advanced placement

API: Academic Performance Index (California)

ASBO International: Association of School Business Officials International

ASC: Alliance for School Choice

ASCD: Association for Supervision and Curriculum Development

AT: assistive technology

ATE: Association of Teacher Educators

AYP: adequate yearly progress

BD: behavioral disorder

BICS: Basic Interpersonal Communication Skills

BICSE: Board on International Comparative Studies in Education

BIP: behavior intervention plan

BOCES: Board of Cooperative Educational Services

BRT: Business Roundtable

CAD: computer-aided design

CAHSEE: California High School Exit Examination

CAI: computer-assisted instruction

CALP: Cognitive Academic Language Proficiency

CAPT: Connecticut Academic Performance Test

CAT: California Achievement Tests

CBE: Council for Basic Education

CBEST: California Basic Educational Skills Test

CBO: community-based organization

CCSSO: Council of Chief State School Officers

CEC: Council for Exceptional Children

CED: Committee for Economic Development

CER: Center for Education Reform

CFR: Code of Federal Regulations

CK: Core Knowledge

CMI: computer-managed instruction

CMO: charter management organization

CMT: Connecticut Mastery Test

CP: cerebral palsy

CRC: community resource center

CRT: criterion-referenced test

CSAP: Colorado Student Assessment Program

CSD: community school district

CSR: class size reduction

CTBS: Comprehensive Test of Basic Skills

CTE: career and technical education

CTT: collaborative team teaching

Dakota STEP: Dakota State Test of Educational Progress

D.A.R.E.: Drug Abuse Resistance Education

DBQ: document-based questioning

DD: developmentally delayed

DEAR: Drop Everything and Read

DHH: Deaf/Hard of Hearing

DI: differentiated instruction; Direct Instruction

DIBELS: Dynamic Indicators of Basic Early Literacy Skills

DIRT: Daily Individual Reading Time

DL: distance learning

DO: district office

DSTP: Delaware Student Testing Program

ECE: early childhood education

ECS: Education Commission of the States

ED: emotionally disabled; emotional disturbance

EDY: educationally disadvantaged youth

EFL: English as a foreign language

EI: emotional intelligence

EL: English learner

ELA: English language arts

ELD: English language development

ELL: English language learner

ELP: English language proficiency

EMO: educational management organization

EOC: end of course

EOG: end of grade

ERIC: Education Resources Information Center

ESEA: Elementary and Secondary Education Act

ESL: English as a second language

ESOL: English for speakers of other languages

ESY: extended school year

ETS: Educational Testing Service

FAPE: free appropriate public education

FBA: functional behavioral assessment

FCAT: Florida Comprehensive Assessment Test

FEP: fluent-English-proficient

FERPA: Family Educational Rights and Privacy Act

FIMS: First International Mathematics Study

FIP: full inclusion program

FTE: full-time equivalent

FVR: Free Voluntary Reading

GATE: Gifted and Talented Education

GED: General Educational Development

GEE: Graduation Exit Examination (Louisiana)

GHSGT: Georgia High School Graduation Tests

GPA: grade point average

GRE: Graduate Record Examinations

HOTS: higher order thinking skills

HOUSSE: High, Objective, Uniform State Standard of Evaluation

HQT: highly qualified teacher

HSPA: High School Proficiency Assessment (New Jersey)

HSTW: High Schools That Work

IB: International Baccalaureate

IDEA: Individuals with Disabilities Education Act

IEA: International Association for the Evaluation of Educational Achievement

IEP: Individualized Education Program

IES: Institute of Education Sciences (U.S. Department of Education)

IGOs: Instructional Goals and Objectives

IHE: institution of higher education

IQ: intelligence quotient

IRA: International Reading Association

ISAT: Idaho Standards Achievement Tests; Illinois Standards Achievement Test

ISS: in-school suspension

ITBS: Iowa Tests of Basic Skills

ITED: Iowa Tests of Educational Development

ITP: Individualized Transition Program

ITV: instructional television

JTPA: Job Training Partnership Act

K–12: kindergarten through 12th grade

K–16: kindergarten through the end of a four-year college

KIPP: Knowledge Is Power Program

LD: learning disability

LEA: Local Education Agency

LEAP: Louisiana Educational Assessment Program

LEP: limited-English-proficient

LRE: least restrictive environment

LST: Life Skills Training

MAARS: Mississippi Assessment and Accountability Reporting System

MAP: Maine Assessment Portfolio; Missouri Assessment Program

MAT: Metropolitan Achievement Tests

MCAS: Massachusetts Comprehensive Assessment System

MEA: Maine Educational Assessment

MEAP: Michigan Educational Assessment Program

MENC: National Association for Music Education

MH: multiply handicapped

MI: multiple intelligences

MSA: Maryland School Assessment

MTAS: Minnesota Test of Academic Skills

NABE: National Association for Bilingual Education

NAEA: National Art Education Association

NAEP: National Assessment of Educational Progress

NAESP: National Association of Elementary School Principals

NAEYC: National Association for the Education of Young Children

NAGB: National Assessment Governing Board

NAIS: National Association of Independent Schools

NAPCS: National Alliance for Public Charter Schools

NAS: National Academy of Sciences

NASBE: National Association of State Boards of Education

NASDC: New American Schools Development Corporation

NASDSE: National Association of State Directors of Special Education

NASP: National Association of School Psychologists

NASSP: National Association of Secondary School Principals

NBES: National Board for Education Sciences

NBPTS: National Board for Professional Teaching Standards

NCATE: National Council for Accreditation of Teacher Education

NCEA: National Catholic Educational Association

NCES: National Center for Education Statistics

NCHE: National Council for History Education

NCHSCT: North Carolina High School Comprehensive Tests

NCLB: No Child Left Behind Act

NCSL: National Conference of State Legislatures

NCSS: National Council for the Social Studies

NCTE: National Council of Teachers of English

NCTM: National Council of Teachers of Mathematics

NDSA: North Dakota State Assessment

NEA: National Education Association; National Endowment for the Arts

NECAP: New England Common Assessment Program

NEH: National Endowment for the Humanities

NEKIA: National Education Knowledge Industry Association

NERPPB: National Educational Research Policy and Priorities Board

NGA: National Governors Association

NHEIAP: New Hampshire Educational Improvement and Assessment Program

NICHD: National Institute of Child Health and Human Development

NIFL: National Institute for Literacy

NLNS: New Leaders for New Schools

NPEP: Nevada Proficiency Examination Program

NRC: National Research Council

NRP: National Reading Panel

NRT: norm-referenced test

NSBA: National School Boards Association

NSDC: National Staff Development Council

NSF: National Science Foundation

NSLP: National School Lunch Program

NSTA: National Science Teachers Association

OBE: outcome-based education

OCD: obsessive-compulsive disorder

OCR: Office for Civil Rights (U.S. Department of Education)

OSAS: Oregon Statewide Assessment System

OSEP: Office of Special Education Programs (U.S. Department of Education)

OT: occupational therapy

OTL: opportunity to learn

PAWS: Proficiency Assessments for Wyoming Students

PBIS: Positive Behavioral Interventions and Supports

PDD-NOS: pervasive developmental disorder not otherwise specified

PDK: Phi Delta Kappa

PEN: Public Education Network

PI: Program Improvement

PISA: Program for International Student Assessment

POWER: Positive Outcomes While Enjoying Reading

preK: prekindergarten

Project STAR: Student/Teacher Achievement Ratio

PSAE: Prairie State Achievement Examination

PSAT: Preliminary SAT

PSSA: Pennsylvania System of School Assessment

PT: physical therapy

PTA: Parent Teacher Association

PTO: parent teacher organization

R&D: research and development

RFP: request for proposals

RRC: Regional Resource Center

SARC: School Accountability Report Card

SAT: a college admission test

SAT-9: Stanford Achievement Test Series, Ninth Edition

SBDM: school-based decision making; site-based decision making

SBM: school-based management; site-based management

SDM: shared decision making

SDRT: Stanford Diagnostic Reading Test

SEA: state education agency

SED: state education department

SES: socioeconomic status; supplemental educational services

SFA: Success for All

SIG: State Improvement Grant

SIMS: Second International Mathematics Study

SIP: School Improvement Program; State Improvement Plan

SLC: small learning community

SOL: Standards of Learning (Virginia)

SQUIRT: Sustained Quiet Uninterrupted Reading Time

SREB: Southern Regional Education Board

SSC: school site council

SSR: Standardized Sustained Reading Time; Sustained Silent Reading

STAR: California Standardized Testing and Reporting Program

STARS: School-based Teacher-led Assessment Reporting System (Nebraska)

STW: school to work

SURR: Schools Under Registration Review (New York)

SWAS: school within a school

TAG: Talented and Gifted

TAKS: Texas Assessment of Knowledge and Skills

TAP: targeted assistance program

TC: Teachers College, Columbia University

TCAP: Tennessee Comprehensive Assessment Program

TEAC: Teacher Education Accreditation Council

TFA: Teach For America

TIMSS: Trends in International Mathematics and Science Study

TOEFL: teachers of English as a foreign language; Test of English as a Foreign Language

TPR: Total Physical Response

U-PASS: Utah Performance and Assessment System for Students

USDOE: U.S. Department of Education

USOE: U.S. Office of Education

USSR: Uninterrupted Sustained Silent Reading

VLS: virtual learning system

WASL: Washington Assessment of Student Learning

WV-MAP: West Virginia Measures of Academic Progress

About the Author

Diane Ravitch is a historian of education. She is Research Professor of Education at New York University and a senior fellow at the Brookings Institution in Washington, D.C., and at the Hoover Institution at Stanford University.

She is the author of numerous histories of U.S. education, including *The Language Police: How Pressure Groups Restrict What Students Learn* (2003); *Left Back: A Century of Battles Over School Reform* (2000); *The Troubled Crusade: American Education, 1945–1980* (1983); and *The Great School Wars: A History of the New York City Public Schools* (1974). She is also coeditor, with her son Michael, of *The English Reader* (2006), an anthology of classic English literature. This is a companion volume to *The American Reader*, which she edited in 1990. She has edited 15 books and written more than 400 articles and reviews for scholarly and popular publications. Her books and articles have been translated into many languages, including Chinese, Polish, Arabic, Spanish, Swedish, and Japanese.

She served as assistant secretary in charge of research in the U.S. Department of Education in the administration of George H. W. Bush and was appointed to the National Assessment Governing Board by President Bill Clinton. Before entering government service, she was Adjunct Professor of History and

Education at Teachers College, Columbia University. In 1988, she was one of the principal writers of the K–12 history/social science curriculum for the state of California, which is still in use.

In 2005, she received the John Dewey award from the United Federation of Teachers in New York City. She was elected to membership in the National Academy of Education (1979), the Society of American Historians (1984), the American Academy of Arts and Sciences (1985), and PEN International.

She has received honorary degrees from Williams College, Reed College, Amherst College, the State University of New York, Ramapo College, St. Joseph's College of New York, Middlebury College Language Schools, and Union College.

A native of Houston, she is a graduate of the Houston public schools. She received a BA from Wellesley College in 1960 and a PhD in history from Columbia University's Graduate School of Arts and Sciences in 1975. She lives in Brooklyn, New York.